C000268729

THE PICCADILLY TUBE

Mike Horne

Capital Transport

First published 2007

ISBN 978-1-85414-305-1

Published by Capital Transport Publishing
PO Box 250, Harrow, Middlesex, HA3 5ZH

Printed by CS Graphics, Singapore

Photographic credits

BAA Ltd 138, 139

Capital Transport collection 4, 19 top, 21 top, 26 bottom, 27, 29 top, 45, 64, 69, 70, 72 top, 93, 106, 117, 122, 124, 129, 131, 135

M A C Horne collection 22, 26 top right, 29 bottom, 33, 98 top, 121

Hulton Getty 80/81

Alan A Jackson 108

London's Transport Museum, Transport for London 16, 19 bottom, 21 bottom, 23, 24/25, 26 top left, 29 centre, 30, 34–40, 44, 47, 50–53, 55, 56, 59-63, 66-68, 71, 72 bottom, 73, 74, 76/77, 78, 79, 82, 83-92, 94, 95, 97, 98 bottom, 99, 101–105, 107, 109, 110, 112, 114, 120, 123

London Underground Ltd 140

Photomatic Ltd 96

The author and publisher would like to thank Antony Badsey-Ellis, Sue Dixon and Brian Hardy for reading the manuscript and making useful suggestions, and Antony Badsey-Ellis for compiling the index.

CONTENTS

Views of Earl's Court and Piccadilly Circus shortly before the Edwardian tube building boom got under way.

ORIGINS

The Piccadilly Line is typical of London Underground's deep level tubes. Originally built as a strictly urban enterprise it has extended at each end into the green fields of Middlesex helping to generate London's modern suburbs. At the west end of the line extension has taken place using facilities already provided by other, full size railways, one of them a main line company, the other still part of the Underground family. Before opening it faced the usual difficulties in raising finance and had a troublesome (but quite normal) gestation, to which American push and knowhow came to the rescue. It also has its share of historical anomalies, not least the third-of-a-mile central London branch (now closed) to a station once known as Strand, and later as Aldwych. It is a most cosmopolitan Underground line. The sheer variety of locations served – the world's third busiest airport at Heathrow, the museums and academic institutions of South Kensington and Bloomsbury, the semi-detached suburbia of Middlesex, the Victorian inner London bedsits and the former 'hub of the Empire' at Piccadilly Circus – produces a unique mixture of users.

When opened in 1906 the Piccadilly was London's longest tube line, 7.9 miles separating the termini at the built-up fringes of the metropolis, at Finsbury Park in north London and Hammersmith in the west. Some 18 stations were opened then, and four more in 1907 including the Strand branch. Today, the Piccadilly Line is the second longest line covering some 44.3 route miles with 51 stations. It is not entirely coincidental that the Piccadilly still serves London's built-up fringes – now at Cockfosters, Uxbridge and Heathrow – the London built-up boundary having shifted outwards hand in hand with the line's own growth.

The history of today's Piccadilly Line is complicated by the section west of Hammersmith, almost entirely constructed by other railways and only later becoming part of the Piccadilly Line. Indeed standing at, for example, Turnham Green today and watching the procession of Piccadilly Line trains thundering through, it is hard to imagine the scene a century ago where the occasional trains might be a District to Whitechapel, a Metropolitan to Aldgate, a London & South Western to Waterloo, or perhaps a Midland goods train to Kensington.

But the heart of the present-day Piccadilly is the original deep level tube section through central London, where hints to the line's early history are given by the sharp curves at Holborn and South Kensington. Proceeding from Finsbury Park, at Holborn the alignment swings sharply from south to west (from Kingsway to Great Queen Street). East of South Kensington the tunnels tortuously follow the street pattern to join the general alignment of the District Line, continuing directly underneath until surfacing between West Kensington and Barons Court. One would be correct in assuming that these features are in some way related to the line's historical origins, and in fact there were three quite separate railway schemes involved: one north-south through Holborn; an east-west line under Piccadilly and a duplicate line sponsored by the District Railway.

The north-south scheme was promoted as the Great Northern & Strand Railway (GN&SR), incorporated by an Act of Parliament of 1899. This was to run from Wood Green to the area now called Aldwych; the actual terminus was to be at Stanhope Street, just north of the present junction of Aldwych and Kingsway. The promoters had originally intended to go only as far south as High Holborn, but, with the new London County Council scheme to redevelop the area, an extension was felt justified underneath the proposed north-south street, Kingsway, as far as the point where it joined Aldwych, the other new main road. The London County Council imposed severe restrictive clauses in the Act, requiring that the southern portion of the line was not to be built without their consent, intended to enforce compliance with their overall objectives in relation to the prestigious Kingsway development.

Like all the early tube lines, much of the tunnelling of the Piccadilly Line was to take place under existing streets, minimizing expensive easements or property purchases. However, much of the route of the GN&SR ran beneath existing railway right of way directly under the Great Northern Railway (GNR) main line into King's Cross, since it was one of several initiatives designed to relieve the congestion on that railway in the inner suburbs. Although the GN&SR was nominally independent, it had the 'concurrence' of the GNR. The section south of King's Cross was intended to help distribute traffic more easily and reduce congestion at the great terminus itself.

The GN&SR seized the opportunity presented by the success of the operation of the City & South London and Waterloo & City Railways, which had been constructed as electrically operated deep tube lines built without significant disruption at street level. The former line (opened in 1890) had used tube tunnelling techniques on a large scale and showed beyond doubt that tube railways were going to revolutionize transport in London. The much grander Central London Railway (CLR) was in course of construction (it was to open in 1900) but had already shown that considerable advances in tunnelling techniques were possible. The future of tube railway development looked very good.

The GN&SR was thus to be built as an electric railway, just over six miles long, in twin tubes of around 12 feet in diameter (21 feet at stations). It was to run mostly beneath the GNR, on its eastern side. Stations were to be at Wood Green, Hornsey, Harringay, Finsbury Park, Holloway, York Road, King's Cross, Russell Square, Holborn and Strand (as Aldwych was called for a few years after opening). Caledonian Road and Gillespie Road stations were authorized later. It was intended that the GN&SR stations at the northern end would be linked by subway or bridge to the adjacent GNR stations.

The power station was to be on Great Northern land near the junction of Gillespie Road and Drayton Park; the maintenance depot would have been at Wood Green. Although the railway was intended as a supplement to the existing GNR no provision for through running of trains was to be made. Notwithstanding the considerable planning and expense incurred, the scheme was unsuccessful in raising capital and there was little activity until 1901: disappointing but quite usual.

Before looking at the next component of the formative Piccadilly Line, it is necessary to look at some other railways in west London in order to set the context. In particular, the activities of the rapidly expanding Metropolitan District Railway (the 'District') are most important, as that company was to provide the springboard for further western expansion of the Piccadilly many years later.

The Metropolitan Railway from Farringdon to Paddington opened in 1863 and constituted the first part of what is now the Circle Line – indeed, it was the first component of the London Underground. Another section opened, from Edgware Road to Gloucester Road on 1st October 1868, extending to South Kensington on Christmas Eve 1868. On that date the Metropolitan's trains also inaugurated services on the first section of the District Railway through its end-on junction at South Kensington, trains running from Moorgate (then Moorgate Street, the Metropolitan having got there in 1865) to Victoria and Westminster Bridge. Mansion House was reached in 1871 and the circle was completed in 1884.

The first incursion towards West London was on 12th April 1869 when a shuttle service operated on one track between Gloucester Road and West Brompton. A separate District tunnel from Gloucester Road to South Kensington opened in 1870, allowing through services to operate from Blackfriars to West Brompton, which services were supplemented by trains from the High Street Kensington direction in April 1880. From junctions near what is now Earl's Court, the District opened a link to the West London Railway's Addison Road station (now Olympia) in February 1872 and another branch to West Kensington and Hammersmith on 9th September 1874.

The three western spurs, and the east-facing junction to both High Street Kensington and the District route to the City, created an important railway interchange at Earl's Court which continues to this day. The western spurs were to provide a springboard for further expansion to the west and south west, especially after the Metropolitan District parted company financially from the Metropolitan in 1871.

The District Railway had itself grown by the turn of the century to a major city railway owning the southern side of the Inner Circle line, and had also spawned a considerable suburban network in west and south-west London extending to Wimbledon, Richmond, Ealing and Hounslow. Assorted other services also fed in via Addison Road. It is important to remember that this was a steam-operated and conventionally signalled system increasingly unable to cope with the rising traffic, the majority of which descended on central London from the west through Earl's Court.

The District recognized that the new technologies for tube tunnelling and electrification could alleviate congestion and promote its further development. It also knew it had to protect its traffic from the immediate plethora of independent tube companies that were being built or promoted (for which the immediate remedy was fare cutting, contributing further to its dire financial position). The District believed the solution lay in the construction of an 'express' tube line beneath its existing railway between Earl's Court and Mansion House. The necessary powers were obtained in an Act of Parliament of 6th August 1897.

The District's express railway was to consist of twin cast-iron tubes of up to 12ft 6ins diameter (25ft at stations). There was to be a junction with the main District Railway just east of Earl's Court, with the tubes thence at deep level under the existing line for nearly five miles, to the City terminus beneath Mansion House Station. Just one intermediate station was proposed, at Charing Cross (now Embankment).

The Act stated that the new railway would be worked by electricity or cable traction, but it also sanctioned the working of the rest of the District by electricity if it so chose. The power station would be in Fulham, at one of three possible sites near Parsons Green or Walham Green. The capital for the deep level line was £1.2 million, to be raised by new ordinary shares, with a further £400,000 permitted as a mortgage on the new line. Valuable though this line was expected to be, the financial burden would be a major one. In the nature of things, no work was actually done.

Simultaneous with the authority to build the District deep level line was the passing of an Act authorizing yet another tube, the Brompton & Piccadilly Circus Railway (B&PCR). This incorporated an independent company to build a deep level tube line from South Kensington via Hyde Park Corner to Air Street, Piccadilly Circus – and so began another strand to the Piccadilly Line's history. The capital was £600,000 in £10 shares and borrowing on mortgage of £200,000. Among the original B&PCR promoters were included C.G. Mott, the Chairman of the pioneering City & South London Railway and the recently retired Superintendent of the Line of the London & North Western Railway, G. P. Neele. Railways along this attractive corridor had been promoted as long ago as 1872, though to no effect.

The B&PCR Act had been gained against the opposition of the unsuccessful City & West End Railway, which would have started at Hammersmith, and run via Addison Road, Kensington Church, Albert Hall, Knightsbridge, Hyde Park Corner, St James's and Piccadilly Circus, and thence via Trafalgar Square to Cannon Street. This railway's promoters were associated with the Central London Railway, a serious competitor to the District which raised vigorous opposition. The B&PCR project, on the other hand, was likely to introduce new traffic to the District Railway's suburban branches, had a complementary alignment, and was in any case the lesser of two evils. The District, ever realists, therefore supported it.

The B&PCR as authorized (between South Kensington and Piccadilly Circus, was not extensive, being just under two miles long. Intermediate stations were to be at Brompton Road, Knightsbridge, Hyde Park Corner, Down Street and Dover Street. Foot subways were authorized at Piccadilly and Dover Street. There was to be a maintenance depot at Yeoman's Row (off Brompton Road), served by a short branch line. The power station was to be near Chelsea, at Swan Wharf (Lots Road), and a cable route was authorized beneath the streets of Chelsea to link the power station with the railway at South Kensington. The Act expressly authorized the B&PCR to enter into agreement with the District Railway about use of its existing foot subway between the station and Exhibition Road to facilitate interchange between the railways. Unsurprisingly, the B&PCR also had difficulty in raising its capital. The District demonstrated its commitment to the B&PCR (and safeguarded its territorial interests) by taking control of the company in 1898, replacing the B&PCR directors with its own on 25th November.

The District and B&PCR companies now being under common ownership presented new opportunities for future inter-working, although combining did not of itself find any money to do any work. On 9th August 1899 the B&PCR obtained a second Act of Parliament which authorized a junction at South Kensington between the B&PCR and the District deep level line, together with necessary adjustments to the levels of the proposed District tube. Additional capital was also authorized, but while the Bill had included provision for a Piccadilly Circus to Long Acre extension this did not succeed. The Act did allow the two companies to enter into an agreement

Great Northern, Piccadilly
& Brompton Railway
showing its component parts

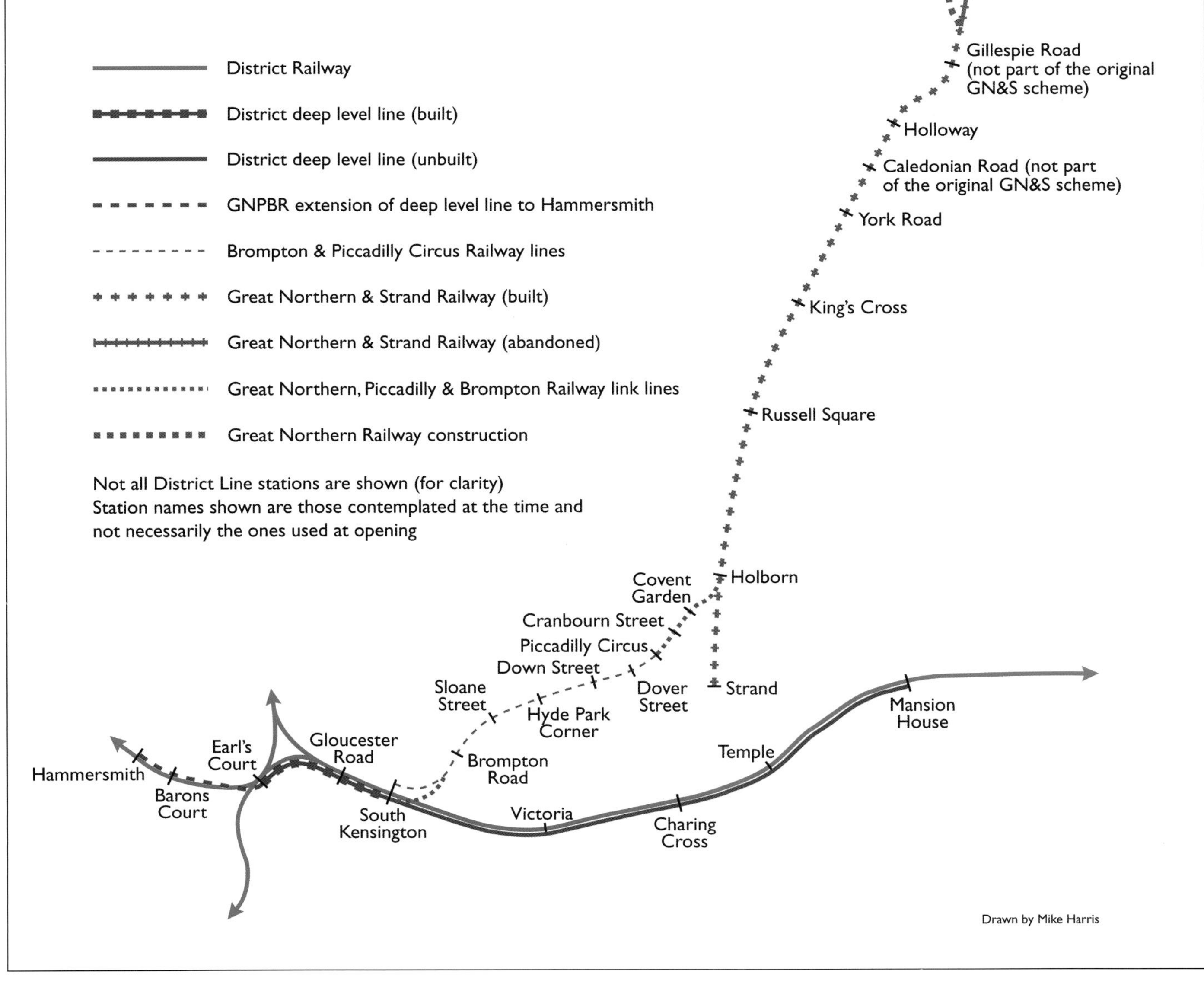
Wood Green
Hornsey
Harringay
Finsbury Park
Gillespie Road
(not part of the original
GN&S scheme)
Holloway
Caledonian Road (not part
of the original GN&S scheme)
York Road
King's Cross
Russell Square
Holborn
Covent
Garden
Cranbourn Street
Piccadilly Circus
Down Street
Dover
Street
Strand
Sloane
Street
Hyde Park
Corner
Brompton
Road
Gloucester
Road
Earl's
Court
Hammersmith
Barons
Court
South
Kensington
Victoria
Charing
Cross
Temple
Mansion
House
District Railway
District deep level line (built)
District deep level line (unbuilt)
GNPBR extension of deep level line to Hammersmith
Brompton & Piccadilly Circus Railway lines
Great Northern & Strand Railway (built)
Great Northern & Strand Railway (abandoned)
Great Northern, Piccadilly & Brompton Railway link lines
Great Northern Railway construction
Not all District Line stations are shown (for clarity)
Station names shown are those contemplated at the time and
not necessarily the ones used at opening
Drawn by Mike Harris

so that the B&PCR could construct the deep level line from its origin at Earl's Court to the junction at South Kensington. It is clear which of the two schemes was now becoming the priority, though the arrangement did not prejudice the eventual prospects for an express tube to the City.

Events were to take a new turn when substantive control of the District Railway was gained by Charles Tyson Yerkes, an American financier who had previously become a multi-millionaire through a lifetime's dealing in American streetcar and city railway companies – not always straightforwardly. At the turn of the century he and his colleagues set about acquiring a number of London's urban railway and tramway companies, most of them (the first was the Charing Cross, Euston & Hampstead Railway) being tube schemes still on the drawing board. Yerkes was in effective control of the District Railway in March 1901 and established the 'Metropolitan District Electric Traction Company' on 15th July 1901; its intention was to provide the finance for electrification and modernization of the District Railway. Since the B&PCR was already under District control it was not long before Yerkes' nominees were placed in charge, a process completed during September 1901.

The B&PCR had already been contemplating continuing its line east beyond Piccadilly. It submitted a Bill in November 1900 for an extension to Russell Square via an interchange with the new Central London Railway at their British Museum station. However, the plethora of tube bills which were emerging – this one included – caused a special parliamentary joint select committee to be appointed, with a brief to consider the long-term appropriateness of the routes being promoted; the committee sat between May and July 1901. The diagram on page 12 gives some indication of the extent of the prevailing tube boom, and this only shows the companies interested in the Kensington–Piccadilly corridor!

The select committee made it clear that it was interested in promoting through routes. The most significant conclusion of the committee was to favour a continuous tube route between the City and Hammersmith via Piccadilly and Kensington, whilst not being concerned about matters of ownership – through running between companies was anticipated. Converging tube junctions were felt undesirable in the light of the signalling technology then available, and this further coloured views.

The effect of this approach was to cause the rejection of the B&PCR's Russell Square proposal, together with a proposed branch line from Brompton Road to the Chelsea station of the West London Extension Railway, via Fulham Road. Instead, the committee recommended that the B&PCR's easterly aspirations be better directed north-eastwards from Piccadilly Circus to the Angel (Islington), via Shaftesbury Avenue, Theobalds Road and Rosebery Avenue – but only if the already authorized section from South Kensington to Piccadilly became a part of the desired 'through' route.

The District Railway was alarmed by the strong support given to competing schemes. The Piccadilly and City Railway, from Piccadilly Circus via Leicester Square, Strand, Fleet Street and Carter Lane to Cannon Street provided obvious competition. The Charing Cross, Hammersmith & District Railway, routed via The Mall, Green Park, Knightsbridge and Hammersmith Road towards Hammersmith, competed with the District and the B&PCR. Although an equally competitive earlier scheme, the City and West End Railway, did not re-emerge in the 1901 session it was known that proposals existed to resurrect the project. This was not good news for Yerkes and his newly formed traction company, and added to the pressures being applied by the successful Central London Railway which was already attracting passengers away from the Inner Circle in worryingly large numbers.

The fear was that a promising 'through route' would emerge, meeting Parliament's requirements but incorporating a competing railway in the Kensington–Piccadilly corridor, effectively sinking the B&PCR and potentially ruining the District. To head off the competition some concession to the committee would be necessary, and seemed likely to require the B&PCR to become part of a through route, by itself or with another. Fortunately the select committee had reported too late for each Bill to progress to Royal Assent during the 1900–01 parliamentary session, so matters were deferred until the 1901-02 session which began in November 1901. This gave Yerkes just enough time to take the necessary action.

Yerkes turned to the still-dormant Great Northern and Strand Railway, already discussed. It is a matter of record that by September 1901 a draft agreement had been drawn up between that railway, its parent Great Northern Railway and the B&PCR, enabling the latter to take over the GN&SR. There was mutual advantage in that capital would now be forthcoming for that tube, and it provided an eastern outlet for the B&PCR. Naturally the Great Northern wanted to protect its own catchment, and the price was the abandonment of the GN&SR tube north of Finsbury Park, both then and for ever more. To ensure that this happened, there were not only protective clauses in the agreements but the main-line railway insisted on building the tube station at Finsbury Park and leasing it to the GN&SR; the Great Northern could repossess the tube station should the GN&SR not honour the agreement, which even extended to banning support for competing schemes. Expansion north of Finsbury Park was now quite impossible without the acquiescence of the Great Northern Railway or its successors.

The agreement was ratified by the GN&SR Board on 6th November 1901, and a second GN&SR Bill was submitted in the new session for its vesting in the B&PCR – and for abandonment of a nearly 3-mile section of line between Wood Green and a point just south of Finsbury Park. A short deviation railway (just over half a mile long) was to be built to link the remainder of the line to a resited low level station at Finsbury Park. Royal Assent was granted on 8th August 1902.

For the 1901–02 parliamentary session two joint select committees were established, Lord Windsor (who had chaired the previous year's session) chairing the committee examining the B&PCR (and competing) ideas. This time there was a wide choice of schemes for railways between Hammersmith and the West End axis. The B&PCR sought powers to forge a physical link to the GN&SR, via Charing Cross Road and Covent Garden, joining the latter at a junction at Holborn. There was also a Central London Railway scheme to convert their line into a 'circle', the new southern side running from Shepherd's Bush to Hammersmith, thence Addison Road, Kensington Church, Knightsbridge, Piccadilly and Strand. The Charing Cross, Hammersmith and District Railway reappeared, following a similar route as far as Hyde Park Corner, thence direct to Charing Cross. The London United Tramways also entered the ring having incorporated a London United Electric Railways Company in November 1901; one of its proposed lines started at Barnes and ran via Hammersmith, Kensington, Hyde Park Corner and Charing Cross. The Piccadilly & City Railway also took heed of the 1901 Committee and projected westwards from Piccadilly to Hammersmith, following the proposed Central London routeing.

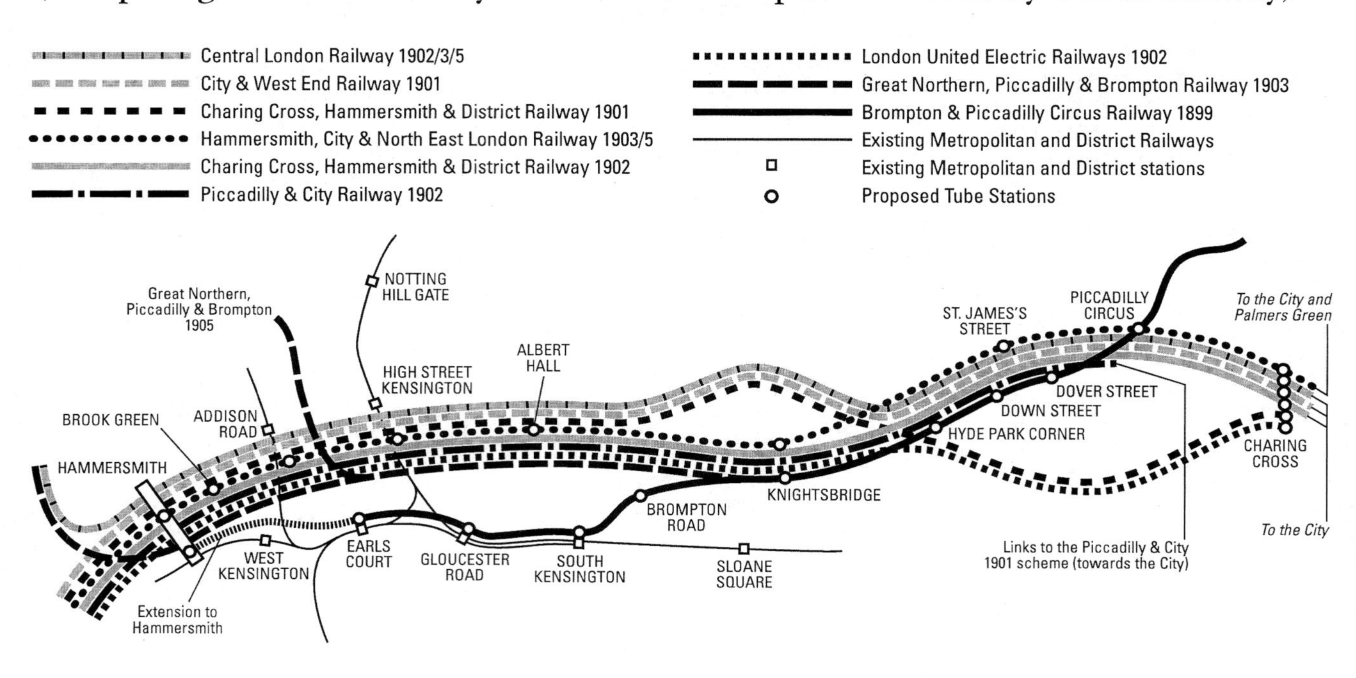

Above is a diagram of proposals for tubes between Hammersmith and central London before the opening of the Piccadilly Tube. For clarity, not all stations are shown.

Yerkes had considerable competition – the success of any of these would ruin his tube's prospects and damage the District. The B&PCR also sought to improve its own viability at the western end. The previous year's proposal for a branch from South Kensington to Chelsea reappeared, this time extended to Parsons Green, where there would be interchange with the District. A link from Piccadilly to Charing Cross was also mooted, but both extensions disappeared during the course of the proceedings.

The progress of these various schemes was highly involved, including significant horse-trading between the sponsors. The Central London and Charing Cross, Hammersmith and District schemes failed. The remaining two schemes were the London United and Piccadilly & City railways; while they were both approved by the Committee (the latter becoming part of the larger Piccadilly, City & North East London Railway) it was on the basis that they had decided to combine resources to build a single continuous route across central London, the various other sections of their original lines being discarded. The two railways had agreed that the Hyde Park Corner to Hammersmith section would be promoted by the London United concern, and the section east of Hyde Park Corner by the Piccadilly, City & North East London company, but Parliament insisted that the whole scheme from Hammersmith to north-east London had to be built as a through route.

After a successful Committee stage it still remained to complete the process of obtaining the requisite powers. Naturally it was the London United concern who continued to promote the remunerative Hammersmith to Hyde Park section. Just as the scheme was in its final stages of progress through Parliament, in September 1902, Yerkes's syndicate – with no outward warning at all – purchased London United Tramways including their railway interests. This precipitated the rapid withdrawal of the London United bill (which near duplicated the B&PCR) and the imposed parliamentary conditions meant that the whole Piccadilly, City & North East London scheme fell too, much to their outrage (so much so that the seeds were sewn for a Royal Commission into London Traffic). It seems Yerkes was to an extent fortunate that relations between London United and the North East London companies had deteriorated, but he was not slow to use it to his advantage when shares became available. So endeth the competition to the B&PCR, and so entered the London United Tramways to the Underground combine.

The B&PCR bill received an uneventful Royal Assent on 18th November 1902. The connection between Piccadilly Circus and Holborn was to be just under a mile long, meeting the GN&SR at a point under Little Queen Street about 80 yards south of High Holborn; the new link would include two new stations, at Leicester Square and Covent Garden. This condemned to branch status the Holborn to Strand section, even though it was located entirely within a redevelopment zone; it is difficult to tell at this stage how its future prospects were really viewed. The now combined railways were renamed – somewhat long-windedly – the Great Northern, Piccadilly & Brompton Railway (GNP&BR). The Act also gave authority for a further station, at Gloucester Road, on the already approved line, and enlargement of that at Knightsbridge. This Act also authorized the B&PCR to take over from the District, by agreement, all the powers of constructing the District deep level line between South Kensington and its junction with the main line just east of Earl's Court, thus forming a continuous railway from Earl's Court to Finsbury Park.

When the District deep level was first sponsored it appears to have been the intention to run through trains onto the main line from a point just east of Earl's Court. In the new circumstances inter-running was not favoured, but there was the need to get the GNP&BR both to Hammersmith and to a depot (since the site at Wood Green was no longer available and the B&PCR site at Yeoman's Row was now inadequate). The solution was to extend the B&PCR to Hammersmith via a new tube station at Earl's Court and dedicated tracks alongside the District, including a new surface station at Barons Court. The GNP&BR would also build a depot on part of the District Railway's existing works near West Kensington (the District was building a new depot for itself in the western suburbs at Mill Hill Park). Hammersmith (as we have seen) was a very suitable traffic centre for an urban railway terminus, connecting with newly electrified (and now commonly owned) London United trams, the District, Metropolitan and London & South Western Railways, and bringing competition to the Central London Railway at its nearby Shepherd's Bush terminus.

The outline details of the B&PCR's western projection were defined in an agreement with the District on 17th April 1902, and confirmed by the District's Act of Parliament of 1903 which also authorized a deviation of the deep level route between Gloucester Road and Earl's Court. The District was required to provide on its own lands access from its main line to the deep level line to allow through running of trains (though it was not obliged to provide the junction more than 20 chains west of the District's West Kensington station). The District's 1904 Act authorized the land purchase necessary to widen its existing line between West Kensington and

1902 map showing the GNP&BR and other Yerkes railways prior to the decision to extend the Piccadilly beyond Earl's Court. After opening, the Piccadilly was shown in yellow on official Underground maps until the start of the First World War. When colour coding returned to the maps in 1919, the colour used was blue and this continued in varying shades until dark blue was settled on when light blue was chosen as the colour for the Victoria Line in the 1960s.

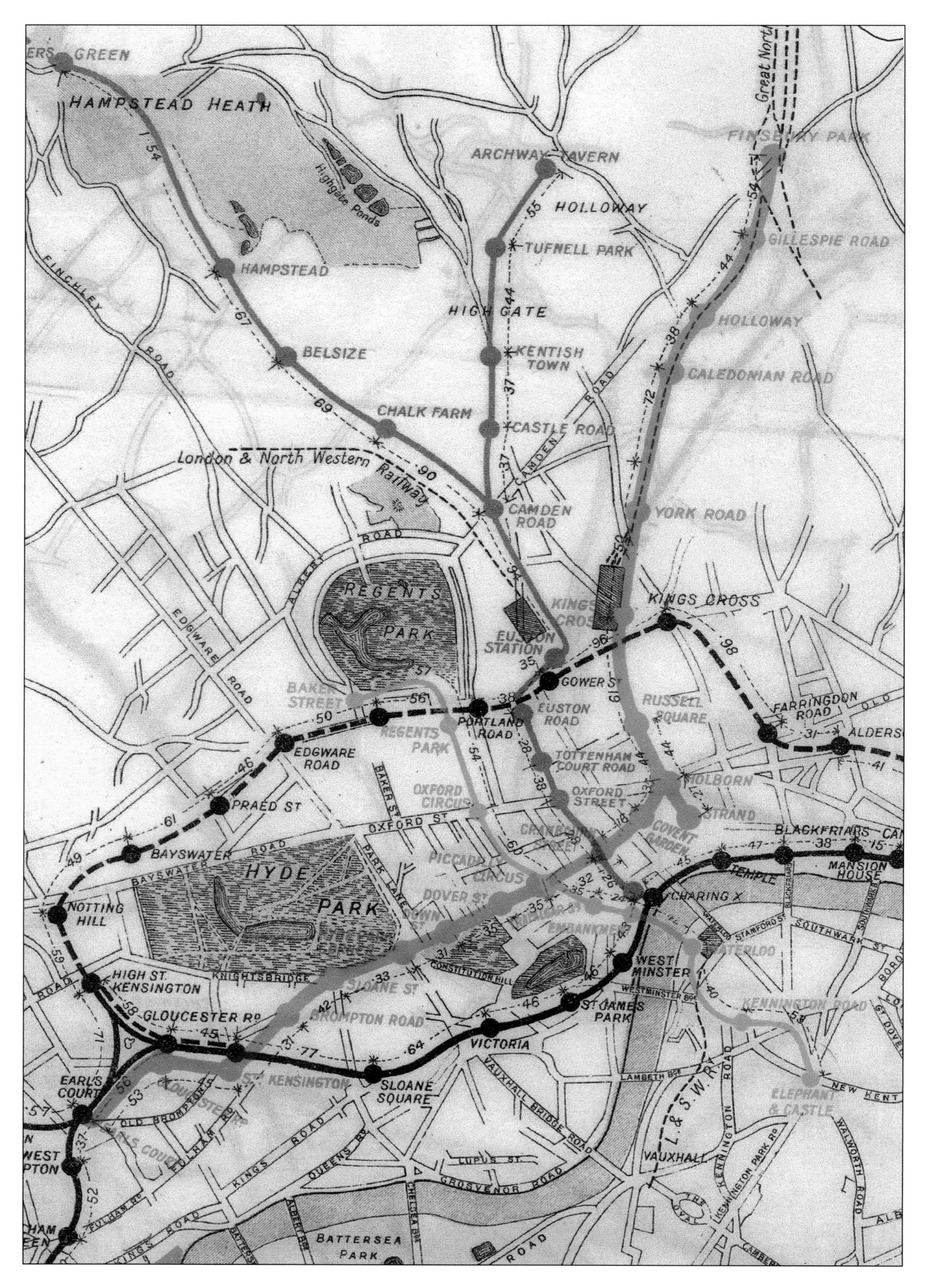

Hammersmith. A further agreement effectively vested the new section of tube between Earl's Court and Barons Court (where it met the District Railway at rail level) in the GNP&BR, who were to build it and pay the District £500 a year for the easement (the District retained running powers – never used – as far as South Kensington). Beyond Barons Court towards Hammersmith the new tracks were to be handed over to the GNP&BR for an annual charge of £12,000, the GNP&BR being required to maintain them as sole user. A formal agreement was embodied in the GNP&BR Act of 1908, after initial agreement in 1905.

Yerkes' expanding aspirations meant that the traction company's capital of £1 million was now wholly inadequate. To the District and GNP&BR portfolio had to be added the unbuilt Charing Cross, Euston and Hampstead Railway (now part of the Northern Line) which had been acquired in November 1901, and the partly built Baker Street & Waterloo Railway (today's Bakerloo Line), added in March 1902. Yerkes had to arrange for considerable additional finance. A start was obtained by establishing a new holding company called the 'Underground Electric Railways Company of London Ltd', or UERL for short. The UERL was registered on 9th April 1902 with a capital of £5 million raised substantially by the banking house of Speyer Brothers. Agreement between the UERL and the traction company was reached on 25th June 1902, following which the assets and liabilities of the latter transferred to the UERL from 8th July 1902, the traction company then being wound up.

With finance in place the scene was now set for a major new tube railway serving north, central and west London. Yerkes' influence had proved to be the turning point for the Brompton & Piccadilly Circus Railway (and the GN&SR), determining its final route through the central area and successfully securing funding.

Map of tunnelling progress in the Piccadilly Circus area.

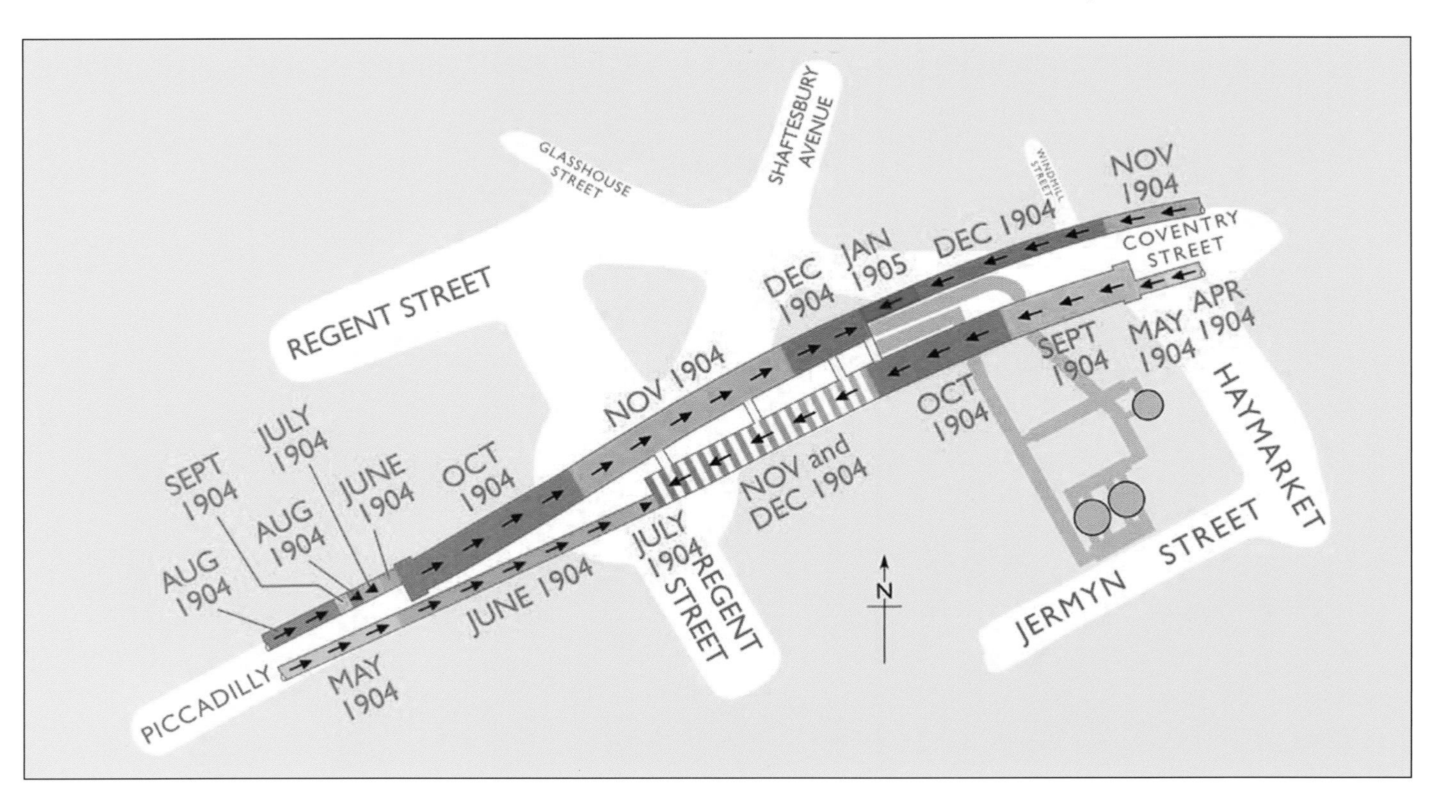

NOTICE.
AS TRESPASSERS
NESTLÉ'S
SWISS MILK
CHOCOLATE
TICKETS
IN
OUT
TICKETS
IN
OUT
NESTLES
SWISS MILK
CLOAK ROOM
LEFT LUGGAGE
LADIES
GENTLEMEN
WASH & BRUSH UP
UNDERGROUND
UNDERGROUND
GREYHOUND RACING
AT THE
WHITE CITY
BOOK TO
WOOD LANE

CONSTRUCTION

The UERL itself was to act as the prime contractor for all the Yerkes' tube lines, resulting in considerable similarity of style and construction technique. It then sub-contracted to a number of firms the building and equipping of the lines. The works on the GNP&BR (uniquely) were split amongst three civil engineering contractors.

The Finsbury Park to Strand section was awarded to Messrs Walker, Price & Reeves, with Mr Alexander Ross as Engineer. Work began in September 1902, and progressed rapidly except on the portion in the Holborn–Strand areas where considerable delay was experienced; at Finsbury Park construction was undertaken by the Great Northern Railway. Half the running tunnels were completed by mid-1903 and most of the rest of the main route by mid-1904, by which time station tiling and platform paving was in hand.

Similarly fast progress was made on the next section from Holborn to South Kensington, also awarded to Messrs Walker, Price & Reeves, but with Szlumper Brothers as the Engineers, who were the first to begin work, on 14th April 1902. However, delays occurred on the portion between Covent Garden and Holborn, the Covent Garden site not being available until 1904. The first station at which tiling could start was Brompton Road, by July 1904. By February 1906 there were still delays to the station tunnels at Holborn; it had also been decided to sink an extra lift shaft at Leicester Square (uniquely, large enough for just one lift).

Cuthbert A. Brereton, with Messrs Walter Scott & Middleton, began construction in July 1902 of the final tube section from South Kensington to the surface east of Barons Court (the District also appointed Brereton the Engineer for the Hammersmith widening, but with Messrs Bott & Stennett as contractor). Work was well advanced by July 1904. This section included the construction of junction tunnels with the authorized District deep level line at South Kensington, which were complete by February 1904, including 30 yards of the District deep level westbound platform to a point beneath the lift shafts. This partial platform was complete by July, including most tiling. This was the only part of the original District deep level scheme to be built, beyond the section ceded to the GNP&BR.

The widening of the District Railway cutting between West Kensington and Hammersmith was completed during 1905, and included complete reconstruction of Hammersmith station. Barons Court station opened for District Railway use on 9th October 1905.

The unsatisfactory progress at Holborn was partly due to difficulty in concluding an agreement with the London County Council – the LCC didn't want the station

Opposite The ticket office at Knightsbridge was typical of those on the GNP&BR and changed little until it was replaced in 1934.

details to be out of character with its overall design for the new Kingsway development (which involved massive slum demolition and constructed of new streets with impressive frontages). Moreover, the railway was clearly unhappy about the track and tunnel layout which had resulted from the link between the B&PCR and GN&SR. The practical effect of the combined GNP&BR was to create a line from Finsbury Park which bifurcated at Holborn, part of the service potentially going to Strand, and part towards South Kensington. At this stage Holborn station would have had three platforms – a single southbound platform (serving both routes) and two northbound platforms (one from South Kensington and one from Strand). This arrangement would clearly restrict capacity on the Hammersmith to Holborn section. It was therefore decided – at a very late stage – to rearrange the station position and tunnel layout, a matter requiring another Act of Parliament which was passed on 4th August 1905.

The Holborn to Strand section was therefore to become self contained, with two separate branch platforms at Holborn; there was to be a single connecting tunnel with the main line north of the station for stock interchange. Initially the western Strand branch tunnel was to be the through line and the eastern tunnel to be the dead end; after yet another change of mind and consequential Act, the dead end platform was squeezed between the two northbound lines and connected to the western tunnel, and the eastern tunnel became the through line. All this caused yet further delay. A crossover linked the two branch tunnels just south of Holborn.

An attempt had been made in the 1902 Bill to extend the Strand branch southwards from the intended site at Stanhope Street to Temple station on the District Railway, but this proposal was thwarted by influential landowners. The 1905 bill proposed an extension from Strand to Waterloo, double track to Surrey Street/Howard Street, thence a single track shuttle. This, too, was largely frustrated although the Stanhope Street–Surrey Street section was authorized allowing the relocation of the Strand terminus 275 yards further south, just beyond the southern margin of the LCC's redevelopment zone. The re-sited station was located near the corner of Strand and Surrey Street on the conveniently shaped site of the Royal Strand Theatre. This establishment, which had seen better days, was closed on 13th May 1905 after the final performance of a short-lived musical, 'Miss Wingrove', which had only been launched on 5th May. It was demolished in 1906 to make way for the tube station which occupied the same footprint and was perhaps more commodious than would otherwise have been the case.

GNP&BR construction methods were similar to those employed on the BS&WR, with running tunnels of cast iron of 11ft 8¼ins in diameter on the straight, and 12ft or 12ft 6ins on curves; station tunnels were 21ft 2½ins in diameter. So far as possible stations were built with approach tracks rising at 1 in 66, and departing tracks falling at 1 in 33, to facilitate the stopping and starting of trains. Much of the tunnelling was undertaken manually using the (by then) conventional Greathead shields. Designed by engineer James Greathead this method of construction involved forcing a tubular steel shield into the ground ahead of the working face of the tunnel and so protecting the miners inside. A ring of tunnel iron was then erected into the newly dug space; then the shield was shoved forward again so the process could be repeated. About a third was done somewhat faster by using the Price rotary excavator, which was similar to a conventional shield system except that at the leading edge the clay was cut away by a massive rotating drum carrying serrated teeth.

By February 1906 ninety per cent of rails and sleepers were in position and the Finsbury Park to Holborn section was almost ready for trains. Between Holborn and Earl's Court there were a few places where contractors were still in possession. Rolling stock for 36 trains was under construction and the contract had been let for the car sheds at Lillie Bridge, with many men at work. Trackside cabling, signalling and lighting work was in hand; substations were nearly ready for their equipment. The lift machinery was in course of delivery.

By July the running and current rails had been laid throughout, apart from a small section at Covent Garden. The car sheds had been finished and were receiving rolling stock at a rate of 15 cars per week. Substations were complete and in operation, except at Hyde Park Corner, which was expected in September. Surface station buildings were proceeding rapidly and it was announced that all would be ready on the main route in January 1907.

In the event the line was opened between Finsbury Park and Hammersmith on Saturday 15th December 1906, by David Lloyd George MP, President of the Board of Trade. A trial service had run from Monday 3rd December 1906 to familiarize staff. Some intermediate stations were not quite ready, and opened later: South Kensington on 8th January 1907, Down Street on 15th March 1907 and Covent Garden on 11th April 1907. The branch from Holborn opened to Strand on 30th November 1907.

Above GNP&BR postcard showing the back of the construction shield and newly erected tunnel behind it.

Below This 1906 poster, announcing to construction staff the imminent operation of electric trains, was uncovered at King's Cross in the 1950s.

The GNP&BR was the second of the UERL tube lines to open, the Baker Street & Waterloo Railway (the 'Bakerloo' as it rapidly became known) having opened on 10th March 1906. Lessons had been learnt from the Bakerloo: there had been problems with the use of universal fares, and on the GNP&BR graduated fares were employed from the start, fares ranging from 1d to 4d in halfpenny steps. Season tickets were also issued, together with some through bookings with other lines. As with the succinct 'Bakerloo' name, a handy abbreviation of the mouthful 'Great Northern, Piccadilly and Brompton Railway' was vital, and it was promoted officially from the start as the 'Piccadilly Tube', though 'Tube' was later suppressed in favour of the title 'Railway'.

The station buildings were all of steel framed construction in a style similar to those on the Bakerloo. The generic layout comprised a two storey building with, on the ground floor, a ticket office, separate lift entrances and exits and access to the spiral stairway. The upper floor housed the lift winding gear. The disposition of staff accommodation, storage and cloakrooms varied according to site conditions and could be found on ground or first floor levels or in the basement depending on space. The exteriors were clad in ruby-red glazed terracotta blocks and the first floor was characterized by huge arched window openings, all of which gave the stations a superficially similar appearance and a very distinctive identity. The first floor roofs were flat and were intended to allow future development above. The Central London Railway had already successfully pioneered such developments and the new tubes all marketed the air space as soon as the stations were ready, as it was essential to maximize revenues from these sites at the earliest opportunity. At Knightsbridge the usual fascia design along the road of that name was adapted to a more ornamental form; perhaps such a utilitarian thing as a railway station was acceptable only on sufferance – the rear entrance in Basil Street (still there today) was plain enough.

Arrangements varied at interchange stations. At Hammersmith, Barons Court and Earl's Court, joint station buildings were erected in the prevailing District Railway architectural style. The platforms at Hammersmith comprised a central island for departures and side platforms for alighting; these were all exceedingly narrow. Interchange with the District was only available via the ticket hall (the case also at Barons Court where the Piccadilly had its own island). At Gloucester Road and South Kensington, the Piccadilly's stations were built next to the existing District Railway premises, and there was interconnection between the ticket halls; no direct interchange was available between platforms. At Piccadilly Circus the station building was shared with the Bakerloo, though separate lifts for each line were provided – there was also low level interchange. For some reason the companies were desperate to keep traffics separate and two stairways were provided in the single stairshaft, the Bakerloo's intertwined with the Piccadilly's, with no connection between the stairs or each railway's access passages – an extremely unusual arrangement probably consequent on the Bakerloo station being partly complete by the time work on the Piccadilly began. On the other hand at Leicester Square all facilities were shared with the soon-to-be-opened Hampstead Railway. No interchange was made at Holborn with the close-by Central London station at British Museum, a major omission considering the railways crossed here; a theoretical interchange was later introduced at street level, evidenced by through tickets. British Museum (planned in the 1890s) was a logical enough site at the time, but the construction of Kingsway made the corner of Kingsway and High Holborn much more attractive to the GNP&BR. At King's

Above Hammersmith Broadway in the Edwardian era. The horse bus nearest the camera is alongside the entrance to the Piccadilly and District Railway station.

Left Hammersmith Broadway station (east end) around the time of the GNP&BR opening. All platforms were quite narrow – the centre platform was for boarding passengers. The District station was to the left of the screen and the signal box served both railways. In 1910 an additional entrance was opened at this end of the station.

Above The *Daily Graphic* was keen to show Londoners pictures of the new tube at the time of opening, and included the platforms at Holloway Road with the striking tile design.

Above right Brompton Road station platform at about the time of the GNP&BR opening.

Cross the station was close to the main line station of that name, and a short walk from St Pancras. Low level interconnection was made with the City & South London Railway which extended through King's Cross the following year; at top level a connection was made from the ticket hall to an existing subway connecting the main line station to that of the Metropolitan Railway, whose ticket hall was then on King's Cross Bridge, connecting Gray's Inn and Pentonville Roads.

The Great Northern Railway was in charge of works at Finsbury Park, where the ticket office was constructed directly under the main line station, within a lengthy subway network which led to the Piccadilly and Great Northern & City Railways; the subway and tube platforms were clad in glazed white tiles and were in contrast to other stations on the line.

The UERL took an innovative but consistent approach to decorating the lower levels of its own tube stations. The platforms were nominally 350ft long and the walls were tiled to a height of about 7ft 6ins in a light background colour. This background was bounded at top and bottom by strings of coloured tiles (either one or two colours), with a further string at waist level, dividing the background into upper and lower portions. Above the tiling the ceiling vaults were plastered and painted, but at intervals bands of coloured tiling (just under 2ft wide) were carried right over the ceiling vault and through the platform wall tiling, effectively dividing the wall into lots of 'panels' – widths varied but sections between 11ft and 12ft would not be unusual. In most of these panels, and above the waist level string, a geometrical pattern of coloured tiling was positioned, the exact colours and patterns varying from station to station such that the combination at any one station gave it a unique appearance that regular users would recognize. Some of the panels (usually three per platform) carried the station name which was fired into the tilework in letters 15ins high. The coloured tile strings (but not the patterns) were continued through most low level passageways. The concept had been developed on the Bakerloo and gave the stations a pleasing appearance that conformed to a common theme whilst making each one individual. The effect was completed by the use of brilliant arc lighting, supported by a number of incandescent lamps that doubled up as emergency lights. Arc lights were also used outside stations to illuminate what might otherwise have been very drab-looking stations at night, and making them stand out against the surrounding buildings, illuminated only by gas-lit street lamps.

Some 60 electric lifts were installed at 17 of the 19 stations in tube tunnel, and these were supplied by Otis. Shafts generally had room for two lifts, but some contained three, while one of the shafts at Leicester Square only had space for one. Not all lifts were installed before the line opened and in later years some were removed where traffic permitted, a few redeployed elsewhere. In addition, four hydraulic lifts were provided by the GNR at Finsbury Park, sharing the same hydraulic plant used by the Great Northern & City Railway (which also terminated there and had its own lifts). The Finsbury Park lifts linked platform level with the high level subway directly beneath the main line platforms, and were intended to provide convenient interchange (passengers from the street to the GNP&BR faced long passages and stairs); the lifts had a short life – one pair was replaced by stairs by 1910, and the other pair withdrawn in the 1920s. The lifts at South Kensington were unusual in having two lower landings, the platforms being at different levels to avoid conflicting track layouts at the proposed junctions; the lift operator would have done his best to avoid confusion here but after some years the passengers were directed to leave by the entrance at the first landing (eastbound) and the exit at the second landing. At a few stations the lifts came down between the platforms, providing convenient same-level access, though at the other locations stairs, and in some cases lengthy passages as well, were required by site conditions as the station buildings that housed the lifts were rarely directly above the platforms which usually ran under the road. No lifts were required at the enlarged District Railway surface stations at Hammersmith and Barons Court, nor at Gillespie Road tube station where ramped passages were built because of the relatively shallow tunnel depth.

There were differences in detail between the various stations, such as the manner in which the exterior lettering was executed. Each station advertised the building rights for construction of a superstructure. These two photos, taken very soon after opening, show two station buildings that were superseded by re-sited ticket halls in the 1930s, though the Dover Street entrance to what became Green Park station survived until the 1960s.

At Holloway Road construction began of a moving walkway in the second (unused) lift shaft. This comprised an intertwined up-and-down spiral belt, complete with balustrading and handrail. The inclined belt was covered in teak slats and disappeared underneath fixed platforms top and bottom, where people could get on and off. The drive mechanism was below the bottom landing. The device was produced by the Reno Electric Stairways and Elevator Company with installation in the hands of Aston & Son, but it was not ready at the opening of the line. There is no evidence for the machine ever having entered service and it seems likely the project, probably only intended for demonstration purposes, was quickly abandoned with most of the remains being taken away in 1911. Much of the drive mechanism survived disposal as the lower landing was simply floored over; it was rediscovered in the 1980s and some key components were retrieved for London's Transport Museum.

The Piccadilly Line lifts at Piccadilly Circus showing the general arrangements. Passengers waited here to board lifts and exited from the other end of them. In later years characteristic movable indicators were installed so that the position of the lifts could be determined in the shafts.

LIFTS TO
GREAT NORTHERN
& BROMPTON
3
HAMMERSMITH
EARLS COURT
&
KINGS CROSS
FINSBURY PARK
PRIVATE
3
FINSBURY PARK
4
GEORGE
GRAVES
PICCADILLY RLY
HAMMERSMITH
EARLS COURT
HOLBORN
KENSINGTON
BOOK HERE

At Holloway Road an experimental spiral elevator was planned. Shown here under construction, it appears to be a view immediately below the top landing at one of the points where the spirals passed each other, and before the balustrading was erected.

Above right The elevator was intended to deliver and collect passengers at ticket level within this enclosure, shown here, courtesy of the *Daily Graphic*, closed off and still awaiting commissioning. This view shows where the gate was for entry or exit, at the point where the rising moving track reached floor level before falling away again on its descent. It is taken nearly opposite the previous photo and about 10ft higher up.

In addition to the vertical transport provided at most stations there was a separate shaft containing a fixed spiral stairway. Nineteen exhaust fans were available at various locations to provide ventilation, providing a total capacity of 18,500 cubic feet per minute. The air ducts for these fans often passed up the centre of the stair shafts.

The depot at Lillie Bridge was built on part of the site of the former District Railway works near West Kensington. At first the land was rented to the GNP&BR but the District was keener on sale and in 1908 the sheds and other land used exclusively by the Piccadilly were sold by the District for £165,999. The car sheds had six tracks and, at 1,312ft, were nearly a quarter mile long, enough for four complete trains on each road. Workshops were provided at the southern end. Empty Piccadilly trains had to run on the electrified District lines through West Kensington station to reach their own tracks; although a dedicated back road was mooted between the depot and the exchange sidings near Barons Court, it was never built. Worse still, the District's automatic signalling in the West Kensington area was not completed until 1908 when West Kensington East cabin opened, and the depot access was initially worked as a single line with pilotmen.

Trains at Lillie Bridge depot shortly after the line's opening.

GNP&BR postcard showing the interior of the turbine hall at Lots Road power station, which served all the Yerkes lines.

The power supply from Lots Road generating station was brought in ducts beneath the streets to Earl's Court (superseding the earlier South Kensington proposal). The power was then distributed via cables in each tunnel to the substations at Hyde Park Corner, Russell Square and Holloway Road. In addition the railway received traction current directly from the District's substations at Earl's Court and South Kensington.

Signalling followed the practice on the Bakerloo railway and was broadly similar to that on the District, which had pioneered the system. The line was track-circuited throughout and the majority of signals were automatic, with the track circuits causing the signals to display red or green aspects depending on whether the line ahead was occupied by a train or not. The signals consisted of a single lamp in front of which moved a 2-aspect spectacle operated by compressed air. At each signal a train stop device was fitted which caused the brakes to apply on any train attempting to pass the signal at danger. In addition to these 'stop' signals a few repeaters (showing yellow or green) were provided where siting of stop signals was particularly awkward. At Finsbury Park, York Road, Covent Garden and Hyde Park Corner there were crossovers, and the signalling was controlled from small signal cabins equipped with miniature Westinghouse lever frames and illuminated diagrams showing the location of trains. Similarly there was a cabin at Holborn controlling signalling on the Strand branch and the connection with the eastbound line. Between West Kensington and Hammersmith signalling was controlled from the District Railway signal boxes at West Kensington and Hammersmith, and the signals were of the District's semaphore pattern, though controlled by compressed air that was actuated electrically.

GNP&BR postcard showing the interior of the signal cabin at Hyde Park Corner, where there was a crossover between the lines. The self-winding clock seen here was typical of the type supplied in large numbers to the Yerkes railways and was synchronized with a master clock at the power station. The illuminated line diagram on the left showed the position of the trains. The lever frame in the foreground (supplied by the Westinghouse Brake Company) operated the points and signals on the electro-pneumatic principle and the levers were interlocked with each other to prevent conflicting routes being set up.

The trains were of 'multiple-unit' formation consisting of 72 motor cars and 144 trailers. All the motor cars were equipped with driving cabs at one end. Half the trailers were equipped with driving controls at one end and became known as 'control trailers'. Both kinds of trailer had an open platform at each end with lever-operated swing gates (operated by a gateman) controlling access; entry to the car was gained through a pair of sliding doors from the gated platform and these doors were supposed to be kept closed while the train was between stations. Motor cars necessarily had only one platform, at the trailing end. On control trailers the driving controls were locked when the platform was being used by passengers; while a glazed windscreen on these cars gave the driver some protection, he was still exposed to the dirt and draughts compared with the comfort of a proper driving cab.

Cars were about 52ft long and trailers could seat 52 passengers and motor cars 42; straps were provided for standing passengers. The motor cars had a single large motor bogie requiring the car underframe to be swept up to clear. The equipment compartment was mounted above the motor bogie. In contrast to the other Yerkes tube lines the order for rolling stock was split. Half the trains were built by 'Les Ateliers de Construction du Nord de la France' at Blanc Misseron near to the Belgian border. The others were built by the Hungarian Railway Carriage Company at Györ (known as Raab in German). The cars were shipped to London Docks, thence brought to Lillie Bridge on their own wheels. Both batches were virtually identical and were built mainly of steel, being finished in 'engine lake' (maroon). Inside, the cars were finished in fireproof mahogany veneer. The numbers of different car types could produce up to thirty-six 6-car trains, each capable of splitting into 3-car sets at quiet times, but it was years before trains this long were required; fortunately cars could be run in any formation as long as a driving position was available at either end, and short trains of three, four and five cars became quite normal.

In addition two further trailer cars were built, one by Brush Electrical Engineering and the other by the Metropolitan Amalgamated Railway Carriage & Wagon Co. It is thought these were intended as samples, but they did not enter passenger service, being out of gauge.

Opposite top A French-built motor car of 1906, one of a total of 216 cars delivered for the Piccadilly Tube to enable the formation of thirty-six 6-car trains.

Opposite centre left This view of a pair of car ends shows clearly how the gates worked; the operation of a lever by the gateman (standing between the cars) caused each gate to unfold into the open position. The inter-car barrier was to prevent anyone from falling down between the cars – they lasted until the 1920s and modern equivalents were installed in the 1990s when this safety feature was felt worth reviving. The 'gateman' in this view is a female member of staff employed during the First World War.

Opposite centre right The interior of the original rolling stock a few years after introduction, by which time it had been fitted with advert frames and a line diagram.

Opposite bottom The GNP&BR purchased a pair of battery locomotives to aid construction and for operation of works trains after the current was cut off. The equipment was mounted behind the nearer cab and the batteries slung between.

G N P & B
64

ALLOW PASSENGERS TO ALIGHT FIRST PLEASE

CARPET
IMPORTERS
DESIGNERS

1B. GREAT NORTHERN PICCADILLY & BROMPTON RAILWAY 1B.

Strand (later Aldwych) station opened nearly a year after the rest of the line; this is the Surrey Street frontage and the main entrance was to be the far opening with a retail unit under the arch. The first floor arrangements were later rebuilt.

DEVELOPMENT

The three Yerkes tubes were legally quite separate undertakings. Recognizing that there would be advantages to be gained from operating them as one integrated concern an attempt was made to obtain the necessary powers in 1903 – the Piccadilly seeking powers to become the 'Underground Consolidated Electric Railways' and the other two lines seeking powers to merge with the Piccadilly, which would be leased to the UERL in perpetuity. This move was frustrated in Parliament condemning the tubes to continued independent existence. However, shortly after the Piccadilly sprang into life it became evident that the advantages in working the lines as a single network were too great to be ignored. By 1907 a common rule book had been adopted, certain staff had responsibility that spanned more than one line, administration became pooled and staff travel was extended across the network. A common ticket system emerged quickly, and this included through booking arrangements to neighbouring railways and associated bus and tramway systems. A common map appeared and publicity promoted all three tubes. Quite quickly there was some exchange of rolling stock between the lines to meet differing rates of growth. Everything was done to operate as a single network that was possible without legislation.

The District, with its own alliances and rather different operating practices, remained outside this scheme and continued to endure great financial difficulties, which the Piccadilly was adding to. The District observed that the Piccadilly was abstracting an alarming amount of traffic, especially that in the wedge of London bounded by the Thames and Knightsbridge/Piccadilly. The group Chairman, George Gibb, nevertheless determined that in overall terms the group was benefiting as people enjoyed the new journey opportunities, and in due course the District's traffics did return.

On the main Piccadilly Railway enough rolling stock had been ordered to operate 6-car trains at the busiest times, but when opened a more modest service was provided using a preponderance of 3-car trains running at 3-minute intervals (4½ minutes off-peak). For some years the Piccadilly had considerable excess rolling stock, some of which was used to improve services on other lines. Service levels improved only very slowly – a year after opening, sixteen 3-car trains provided a 4–4½ minute service off-peak, and these were supplemented by eight 5-car trains in the peak to offer a slightly better than 3-minute average service. At the end of 1908 all trains were of 3-cars, 35 trains offering a 2-minute peak service, reducing to a 22-train, 3-minute off-peak service.

Traffic developed at a disappointing rate, partly because of the introduction of electric trams and motor buses during the period of construction, and in the first full year of operation only 26 million passengers were carried against the 60 million anticipated – nothing like enough to pay operating costs, interest on capital and rewards for shareholders. Fresh management talent was brought to bear and aggressive marketing slowly turned the problem around. As part of this an agreement was made with the other independent underground railway operators to jointly promote the network under the name UNDERGROUND, and corporate nameboards and maps started to appear at all stations; the range of through fares to and from other railways was expanded, and local fares were co-ordinated to avoid competition within the group but to compete on reasonable terms with the buses. Season tickets disappeared to make way for the strip ticket (a number of tickets sold at a discount rather like the more recent 'carnet'). Better still, service levels were enhanced to improve attractiveness, last train times co-ordinated and running times reduced. The formula worked.

From 11th October 1909, attempts were made to speed up the peak hour service by introducing skip-stop trains which alternately omitted either Caledonian Road and Gillespie Road or York Road and Holloway Road. This, of course, made it impossible to travel directly between certain of these stations. One train was saved: it was now possible to run the peak hour service with 34 trains, half of which were strengthened to 5-cars again. With the advantages in journey times the skip-stop idea was to spread later – for many years a variety of non-stopping patterns featured on the Piccadilly, though it became renowned as a confusing characteristic of the line until it ceased in June 1947, apart from the non-stop section between Hammersmith and Acton Town.

Like its precursor the theatre, Strand station didn't attract many customers when the short, isolated branch to Holborn opened in 1907. Even when fully revitalized, the Aldwych area was very well served by buses and trams, and both Holborn and Temple stations were close. Strand was only of real use to those travelling northwards, and the need to change at Holborn was a significant disincentive. Although twin tunnels had finally been built, with two dedicated platforms at both stations, three of the four branch platforms were only 250 feet long and even those at Strand were not tiled throughout their length since only 2-car trains were now envisaged and the expense of unnecessary tiling seemed unwarranted. Indeed, at Strand, many low-level passages were also not tiled and were to remain unused throughout the station's life.

Initially each of the branch tunnels could carry a separate shuttle service of 2-car trains, though for a few years shortly after opening occasional trains ran from Strand to Finsbury Park for the benefit of passengers returning from nearby theatres in the evening; these used the trailing junction with the 'main' line north of Holborn and no service in the reverse direction was possible. Even this minimalist provision proved over-optimistic. By no later than March 1908 the normal service operated only in the 'western' tunnel and the 2-car train was reduced to a specially converted single car – this was augmented to a 2-car set during peaks, the spare car being stabled at either Holborn or Aldwych when not in use. Within a few years the branch signalling was removed (saving the cost of a signalman) and the service train was physically 'locked' into one of the single lines (a spare train was kept on the other one). From 1915 Strand was renamed Aldwych. The decline continued. A Sunday service last ran on 8th April 1917 and during the following year the spare train was forsaken when most of the eastern tunnel became disused. The service ran from the western platform at Aldwych to the eastern platform at Holborn and the crossover was replaced by plain track; even so, an impressive 4-minute service in each direction was run for some years. The disused Aldwych eastern platform was used to house National Gallery treasures in the latter years of the First World War. From 16th August 1921 the ticket office at Aldwych closed for good, and automatic machines were substituted. A little later, miniature ticket offices were opened in the lifts; by this means one lift operator could issue and collect tickets as well as operate the lift, cutting staff down to the bare minimum. After these reductions the line settled down to an uneventful future.

Aspirations to combine legally the three Yerkes tubes came to fruition on 1st July 1910; the GNP&BR was officially renamed the 'London Electric Railway' (LER), and simultaneously absorbed the Baker Street & Waterloo, and Charing Cross, Euston & Hampstead Railways. The main benefit was in combining the accounting and capital structure of the tubes: the tracks necessarily remained physically separate. The change made little immediate difference to the public or the mode of operation, except that each tube was formally styled as a 'Line' within the LER rather than a 'Railway'. They became known, respectively, as the Piccadilly Line, the Bakerloo Line and the Hampstead Line – the first two retaining the same names today.

The Underground's first escalator at Earl's Court linked the Piccadilly and District Railways. Advertisements and exhortations to 'stand on the right' came later.

A NEW STAIR LIFT.

THE NEW AUTOMATIC STAIRCASE, NOW WORKING AT EARL'S COURT STATION, WHICH CONVEYS PASSENGERS FROM THE PICCADILLY TUBE TO THE LEVEL OF THE DISTRICT RAILWAY.

An historic event occurred on 4th October 1911 when a pair of escalators was introduced at Earl's Court between the District and Piccadilly lines – the first of hundreds on the Underground. The machines were produced by the Otis Elevator Company and were different from the machines known today, since the models used did not include cleated steps and landing 'combs'. To avoid the danger of taking passengers' feet to the brink of where the steps disappeared into the machine's innards 'Shunt' landings were built, where the balustrading swept across the escalator at an angle, forcing passengers to step off the machine sideways. Shunt landings had always to be used at the alighting end, but at the boarding end passengers could step on directly. The Piccadilly did not itself receive any further escalators until 1928, by which time the use of cleated steps and combs on new machines was universal; older machines were almost all replaced or converted to cleated style, those at Earl's Court being replaced in 1936.

The First World War marked the beginning of a period of pressure on the Piccadilly Line. Even in wartime traffic levels were to rise substantially, and amongst other things served to highlight the shortcomings of the labour-intensive lift system. Until then, an attendant was required in each lift to check tickets, to operate the gates and to operate the lift mechanism. In 1914 an attempt was made to improve the efficiency of this arrangement and at Piccadilly Circus experimental lift control equipment was installed on each of the lift landings. This allowed just two attendants (one at each landing) both to control lift dispatch and check tickets, the attendants in the lifts being withdrawn. Power-operated entrance gates were part of the package (exit gates were already power operated). The experiment was successful and 'landing control' was subsequently extended to many other lift stations on the Underground.

One consequence of the War was the creation of the Underground Group 'pool'. The District Railway (but no other UERL company) was placed under government control at the beginning of the War and was subject to different regulations from non-requisitioned companies; one difference was the ability to pay staff a 'war bonus', which was regarded by the UERL as very unfair on non-District staff doing essentially the same work (by this time the City & South London and Central London Railways and the London General Omnibus Company had each been taken over by the UERL). Government sanction was obtained for all the costs and revenues of all the group's railways and the LGOC to be pooled; this allowed the District's bonus and the LGOC profits to create a bonus from which all staff could benefit. It also made it far easier to manage all of these companies as a single going concern. The scheme was put on a statutory basis from July 1915, backdated to January.

Although the Piccadilly Line initially had rolling stock surplus to requirements, the transfer and use of the spare trailer cars on other lines meant a shortage of train capacity was evident during the War despite a limited number of 6-car trains which began running from 1917. To meet the ongoing shortage, some 40 additional cars were ordered from Cammell Laird in 1919. Delivered in 1920/21, the cars consisted of 20 trailers and 20 control trailers, and were the first production batch on a tube line to embody air-operated doors instead of handworked gates. Single doors were installed at each end of the cars and a pair of doors in the centre, though these were separated by a structural pillar. To work with the new cars, 20 of the French 1906 motor cars were rebuilt with air-operated end doors and centre doors, and the staffing requirement reduced to three – a driver and two guards. The original requirements were driver and conductor, with a gateman at each intermediate pair of gangways. When delivery was complete the entire service could be operated by 6-car trains in the peaks, with 3-cars off-peak.

Opposite This Hungarian car of 1906 was experimentally converted to air-door operation in 1911 by fitting externally hung doors. The conversion was not considered satisfactory and the car was then used only on the Aldwych shuttle, duplicate driving controls being fitted at the trailing end and the air-door mechanism removed.

Below One of the first cars to be built with air-operated doors is shown below. It is a Cammell Laird built air-door control trailer after repainting with cream upper panels (the cars were originally all maroon); the obstructive central pillar between the double doors is clearly visible.

By the early 1920s most of the Piccadilly trains comprised conspicuously unmodernized gate stock, looking increasingly outdated and remaining intensively staffed. Rolling stock modernization was contemplated, including the provision of air doors, but after some experimentation this was not considered cost-effective. A new design of air-door stock was developed for the expanding Hampstead Line from 1923, but with modernization and expansion of the City & South London Railway between 1924 and 1926, and then urgent pressure for replacement stock on the Bakerloo, the Piccadilly had to wait.

In due course an order was placed with the Metropolitan Carriage, Wagon & Finance Co., for 136 cars to replace the Piccadilly's gate stock. The order comprised 47 motor cars, 36 control trailers and 53 trailers, the cars being delivered in 1928/29. This order was supplemented by 20 additional motor cars ordered from the UERL's own Union Construction Company (UCC) at Feltham, and these allowed the French air-doored motor cars (operating the Cammell Laird trains) to be replaced (though two of the French air-door conversion motors were converted for use on the Aldwych shuttle by adding a cab at the trailing ends). In 1930 the 40 Cammell Laird cars were transferred to the Bakerloo Line, being swapped for an identical number of their new cars. Another batch of UCC stock – 53 cars nominally dated 1929 – was also delivered to the Piccadilly, allowing a similar number of the Metropolitan Carriage cars to be transferred to the Hampstead. This re-equipment spelt the rapid demise of gate stock, the last of which ran on the Piccadilly Line in June 1929.

Interior of Cammell Laird trailer around 1920.

Of the six sample trailers sourced in 1922, this example from the Birmingham Railway Carriage & Wagon Co was possibly the most ornate. The car remained in service until 1954 but the most ornate features had long since been replaced by more robust fittings.

1927 control trailer at Lillie Bridge.

Interior of 1929 stock motor car in July 1929. Interior designs had by now been simplified with lighter draught screens. The lamps along the centre of the roof are the emergency lights.

The Aldwych service continued to be operated by single cars of 1906 vintage stock. From around the time of the First World War at least one car with a hand-worked centre door worked the branch (replacing the original single cars). This car, too, was of 1906 origin and was a result of (evidently unsuccessful) experiments in 1911 to provide automatically controlled doors on the main Piccadilly service. It remained in use until 1930 when it was replaced by a further pair of 1906 adapted single cars (one in service, one spare), this time with air-worked centre doors. These cars were also fitted with duplicate brake rigging to mitigate the risk of failure of critical equipment (which was less of a problem with trains of more than one vehicle).

In other respects the Piccadilly Line remained relatively static between its opening in 1906 and the late 1920s. It failed also to attract modernization of its central area stations, a process which was in hand on other lines as a result of suburban extensions and accelerated traffic growth at some locations. There was one notable exception. The reconstruction of Piccadilly Circus station was the first of several architectural masterpieces by Charles Holden which were later to adorn the Piccadilly Line. The station was shared with the Bakerloo Line, but despite its eight lifts was barely able to cope with the mounting traffic, which had increased tenfold since its first year of operation.

The ticket hall at Gloucester Road in the 1920s shows that light traffic had resulted in the ticket office being closed and ticket issue transferred to ticket machines and the lift operator – several stations had a miniature ticket office installed in the lifts.

The new huge new ticket hall at Piccadilly Circus in 1928 contrasted markedly with other stations on the Piccadilly Line. A ticket office was provided, but the use of automatic machines was heavily promoted. This was not altogether successful and Passimeter ticket offices were later added.

Powers to rebuild were obtained in 1923. The new station was constructed during 1924–28 directly beneath the 'circus' roadway. It contained a vast elliptical ticket hall with a flight of five escalators leading to an intermediate landing. From here, a bank of three escalators led to the Piccadilly Line, and another bank of three to the Bakerloo. From the ticket hall, subways and stairs led to several street entrances and to the old ticket hall which was retained to provide additional entrances and a shopping arcade. Plans had originally been tested on a huge mock-up erected in the Empress Hall at Earl's Court and they changed significantly as they developed. Mocked up stairway entrances were also tested on site along the roadways around the 'circus' to check visual impact and effect on circulation. The new station was opened on 10th December 1928, and the lifts were withdrawn (and former station facilities closed) from 21st July the following year. The old entrance became part of a shopping arcade and lasted until the late 1990s when the block was redeveloped.

Traffic levels developed to a different degree at each station, some such as Brompton Road carrying very little and others such as Piccadilly Circus overwhelmed. At some stations the lift 'exits' at street level were soon to fall out of use, either permanently or for periods of the day as traffic dictated. In 1923, for example, the dedicated exits at Finsbury Park, Holloway Road, Caledonian Road, York Road, Aldwych, South Kensington and Gloucester Road were recorded out of use, with traffic entering and leaving at the entrance side. At Finsbury Park, Holloway Road, Aldwych and Gloucester Road the lower level lift 'exits' were also out of use (Covent Garden followed later); arrangements varied slightly over the years.

A poster by E. McKnight Kauffer publicizing the speedier journey between Hammersmith and Acton Town on the western extension of the Piccadilly over former District Railway tracks.

EXPANSION IN THE WEST

As mentioned at the beginning of this book, the history of the Piccadilly Line is complicated by its close links with the District, particularly west of Hammersmith where much of what is now the Piccadilly was built by the District Railway. However, the oldest part of the present-day Piccadilly Line dates back to 1869, and was built by the former London & South Western Railway, one of Britain's principal main line companies.

The District Railway reached the Middlesex riverside town of Hammersmith in 1874, building its station on the south side of Hammersmith Broadway. The Metropolitan and Great Western Railway's joint station (opened in 1864) stood nearly opposite. But there was a third station, Hammersmith Grove, a little further west, which had opened on 1st January 1869. This stood on the London & South Western Railway's line from Addison Road to Richmond via Shepherd's Bush, Hammersmith (Grove Road), Turnham Green, Gunnersbury and Kew Gardens; another station opened on 1st April 1873 called Shaftesbury Road (this is today's Ravenscourt Park, to which it was renamed on 1st March 1888). The line, authorized in 1864, was built largely to protect what the L&SWR regarded as its own territory in South West London, especially the approaches to Richmond which was a major traffic objective in those days. Both the Great Western and Metropolitan Railways were given running powers over the new line west of Hammersmith (the GWR with broad gauge track if it desired, which it never did), and a junction was put in just north of Grove Road that connected to the Hammersmith & City Line.

The line had obvious attractions to the District, pointing due west in continuation of its own line, and with ready-made traffic objectives. In fact joint use of the line suited both companies by stimulating suburban development near the L&SWR-owned line as well as providing additional feeder traffic for the District. The North London Railway was already sharing the section from Gunnersbury to Richmond.

The District obtained running powers in their Act of 1875, which also authorized the 38-chain physical link. The extension started in a covered way beyond the existing District cutting and the remaining quarter-mile climbed steeply at up to 1:43 to Studland Road, where a junction was made with the L&SWR at viaduct level just east of what is now Ravenscourt Park station. District trains started running through to Richmond on 1st June 1877. Trains called at Shaftesbury Road, Turnham Green, Gunnersbury and Kew Gardens. The Metropolitan retaliated by running their own trains to Richmond from 1st October 1877 via their connection with the L&SWR at Hammersmith.

Further expansion quickly followed. A junction was made at Turnham Green and the District Railway built a wholly owned branch line, opened on 1st July 1879, to Ealing Broadway, near to the Great Western Railway station. This served intermediate stations at Acton Green (now Chiswick Park), Mill Hill Park (now Acton Town) and Ealing Common. Although not heavily populated at the time, the area was developing steadily and trains worked through to central London. The District ran through trains over the Great Western to Windsor between 1883–85, via the Great Western station at Ealing Broadway, and considered further western extensions towards Uxbridge; plans, however, remained in abeyance. Meanwhile, the short spur from Earl's Court to West Brompton was changed radically in character, with a busy extension to Fulham and Putney Bridge in 1880 and, jointly with the L&SWR, to Wimbledon in 1889.

The District's extension to Ealing Broadway was the springboard for two branch lines that were later to have a huge impact on the development of the Piccadilly. The first one of these was that to Hounslow, which began life as the Hounslow & Metropolitan Railway; this was originally sponsored by local landowners but was worked by the District until formally taken over by them in 1903. The line was to run between the junction at Mill Hill Park and Hounslow Barracks and was authorized in August 1880. Stations were built at South Ealing, Boston Road (renamed Boston Manor in 1911) and Spring Grove (later Osterley & Spring Grove).

Matters got slightly complicated at the Hounslow end. Before the line opened, the Hounslow & Metropolitan Railway was considering a plan to build a new line towards Whitton via Hounslow High Street which would become the main line, leaving the link to Hounslow Barracks as a branch, for which purpose this section was only built as single track. Opposition saw off most of the proposal but it was decided to build the short link to the High Street station anyway, and this was called Hounslow Town. It was to Hounslow Town that the line opened on 1st May 1883, in advance of parliamentary authority on 29th June. The fact that the authorized terminus served little more than the army Barracks and open farmland (with the line carrying no goods traffic) suggests some logic in the decision, and the line stopped abruptly on viaduct at the edge of the High Street making future intentions fairly clear. The train service, at first running to the City, was rapidly chopped back to Earl's Court and later to Mill Hill Park where enforced changes were needed for the main District services.

The originally authorized terminus at Hounslow Barracks opened on 21st July 1884, though only as a single-track spur from Lampton Junction, which necessarily avoided Hounslow Town station; there were no intermediate stations. Until 31st March 1886 the Barracks service operated as a shuttle to Osterley & Spring Grove which was provided with run-round sidings to the east. This unattractive arrangement could not be sustained and the Hounslow Town terminus closed after traffic on 31st March 1886, with a new station on the Barracks branch (Heston-Hounslow) opening the following day and picking up some of the town traffic. Trains now ran from Hounslow Barracks to Mill Hill Park, and the sidings at Osterley were disconnected; however the line between Lampton Junction and Hounslow Barracks remained single track for many years.

The second of the formative Piccadilly Line branches was the South Harrow line, beginning at its junction with the existing District at Hanger Lane (next to the massive bridge across the Great Western main line).

There had been Bills presented regularly since 1864 for railways through the

Harrow–Alperton axis, and the District had had eyes on Uxbridge since its arrival at Ealing in 1879. Bills continued to be presented regularly from a variety of sponsors (the District included) until 1894, when success was greeted in the form of an Act for the nominally independent Ealing & South Harrow Railway (E&SHR) to build a line as far as Roxeth (near Harrow Hill), from a junction with the District at Hanger Lane via intermediate stations at North Ealing, Alperton, Sudbury Town and Sudbury Hill.

Preliminary work began in 1897 and construction proper started in early 1899. The nature of the yellow clay in the area slowed construction down (not helped by exceptionally wet weather) and extra land was needed to give the banks and cuttings the necessary stability. The Ealing Broadway–North Ealing curve was omitted, so the new line would have to be operated as an alternative branch to Ealing Broadway, which was perhaps unhelpful given the small traffic prospects.

Although practically complete at the end of 1899 the line remained unfinished and unopened – the dire state of the District's financial affairs meant it could not afford to operate near-empty trains. It was during that year that the question of possible District electrification was being addressed and this may have bolstered a decision to delay things, for reasons covered later.

Before the E&SHR difficulties manifested themselves the District's aspiration to reach Uxbridge needed to be sated. As mentioned, the District had already surveyed the route but no bill was deposited at that time. In 1896 practical moves were required and the District deposited a bill for a line making an end-on junction with the E&SHR at Roxeth (or South Harrow, as the District preferred to call its station) and thence to High Wycombe, via Ruislip and Uxbridge (where it would now link with an Uxbridge and Rickmansworth scheme). Great Western opposition saw off the Wycombe section but the line from South Harrow to Uxbridge was authorized in 1897, creating another nominally independent company, the Harrow & Uxbridge Railway (H&UR).

As usual, fund-raising proved difficult, not helped by much of the route being thinly populated. The Metropolitan Railway offered to rescue the scheme (it had itself had eyes on Uxbridge, having promoted an unsuccessful Act in 1881) and with the District's reluctant support, an Act of 1899 was passed which authorized a link from Harrow-on-the-Hill (Metropolitan) to a junction with the H&UR at the then remote Rayners Lane. The Met took over the H&UR powers but the District retained limited running powers for up to three passenger trains per hour between South Harrow and Uxbridge (the South Harrow section, though not on the route from Harrow-on-the-Hill, was still required to be built by the Met). Construction work started in 1901 and took about three years.

It was while this branch was under construction that moves towards electrification of the District were being addressed by installing an experimental system between Earl's Court and High Street Kensington (this came into use during 1900). At some point the decision was made that larger scale experiments would be desirable, and the as yet unopened South Harrow line would provide a useful test bed (the District assumed full control from 1st July 1900). The new line was adapted accordingly.

Two low voltage power rails were installed, one (outer) positive and one (centre) negative, the insulated return avoiding risks of stray currents. A temporary power station was erected near Alperton, the equipment coming from the experimental installation at Earl's Court. Experimental automatic signalling was also installed,

Stations on the South Harrow line were not generally very substantial, but were more than adequate for the traffic in the early 20th century.

using track circuits and pneumatically controlled semaphores. Signal boxes remained only where there were points. A small number of new electric cars were also delivered, and experiments began; success was to be anticipated – nearly all the equipment followed the latest American practice.

The equipment all worked well and the District decided to open the E&SHR line for the Royal Agricultural Show (at the Park Royal showground, between 23rd and 27th June 1903). There had not originally been intended a station between North Ealing and Perivale-Alperton (the 'Perivale' was dropped from 7th October 1910), but showground traffic made it worth while constructing one, and an inextravagant wooden station was thrown up near Twyford Abbey Road, called Park Royal. Unfortunately, treacherous weather caused embankment slips further north which threatened to delay the opening. The District decided to open to Park Royal only from 23rd June, running on a single line basis north of North Ealing to capture most of the promised traffic (though the show had only 65,000 visitors – less than hoped). On 28th June the whole line was opened as far as South Harrow, but services over the Met to Uxbridge had to wait a few more years. Park Royal had been intended as a temporary station but it lasted nearly 30 years as the showground area developed as a major trading estate – the station was later rebuilt on a new site.

Metropolitan trains to Uxbridge began on 4th July 1904 (steam), and 1st January 1905 (electric). The only stations were at Ruislip and at Uxbridge, though halts appeared at Ickenham (25th September 1905), Eastcote and Rayners Lane (26th May 1906), Ruislip Manor (5th August 1912), West Harrow (17th November 1913) and a station at Hillingdon on 10th December 1923. Passenger traffic remained disappointingly low, and most Metropolitan trains ran as shuttles from Harrow-on-the-Hill. There was no service between South Harrow and Rayners Lane until District electric trains ran through from 1st March 1910; the Metropolitan had briefly used the section for electrification tests in 1904, taking power from the District. From 4th October 1910 the Metropolitan ran coal trains to the Harrow & Stanmore company's private gasworks siding just north of South Harrow, which service continued until April 1954 by which time they were something of an inconvenience.

The District was committed to electrification from 1901 and work had begun on the Traction Company's Lots Road power station in March 1902. On 13th June 1905 the Hounslow branch was electrified and electric shuttles from Hounslow were extended from Mill Hill Park to South Acton (by the North London Railway station) over a new District spur built but not opened in 1899. The trunk section from Ealing to Whitechapel was electrified from 1st July 1905, and all main District Railway services, including the Inner Circle and trains over L&SWR tracks to Richmond and Wimbledon, were electrified by November 1905. During 1905–08, the Metropolitan Railway was converted to electric traction for all passenger trains over its routes to Hammersmith, Harrow and Uxbridge. The link at Hammersmith between the Hammersmith & City and the L&SWR was not electrified; from 1st January 1907 a Great Western steam shuttle was laid on, running between Notting Hill & Ladbroke Grove and Richmond.

The power station at Lots Road, Chelsea, opened in 1905 to supply electric current to the Yerkes railways.

Traction power to the west end of the District was distributed from substations at South Kensington and Earl's Court (each shared with the Piccadilly), Hounslow Town, Mill Hill Park, Ravenscourt Park and Sudbury Town. Signal cabins were provided at most District stations in steam days, and sometimes between stations where there were junctions or traffic was heavy. When automatic signalling was introduced the old signal cabins were generally abolished, with new signal cabins, each with an electro-pneumatic lever frame installed. At some locations – especially west of Acton Town – the former cabins and frames were adapted for operation with track circuits, usually with the points operated mechanically but signals electro-pneumatically.

In addition to its new station at Barons Court, the District improved passenger facilities in parallel with electrification. A new station called Northfield (Ealing) opened on 16th April 1908 and this was renamed Northfields & Little Ealing on 11th December 1911. The excellent location of the disused Hounslow Town station, coupled with negligible traffic growth on the Barracks section, caused its brief return to use from 13th June 1905. To avoid having to operate two branches in Hounslow, the Barracks (single) line was served via a new and very sharp curve at Kingsley Road to serve Hounslow Town, trains to and from the Barracks and Mill Hill Park having to reverse. This highly inconvenient arrangement was abandoned on 2nd May 1909 when the through line was re-opened and the Hounslow Town terminus was finally abandoned, a new double track station at Kingsley Road (also called Hounslow Town) replacing it. The site of the first Hounslow Town station was eventually used for a LGOC bus garage and bus station. The line between the new Hounslow Town station and Heston-Hounslow was doubled from 24th April 1910 but it was another 16 years before double tracks reached the Barracks. Some improvements were made at Heston-Hounslow itself in late 1912; the single track platform was removed and replaced by a double track island further to the east, the double line continuing a further few hundred feet towards Hounslow Barracks, together with a new signal box – an arrangement permitting the abolition of the single-line 'staff' working. A crossover at the eastern end and new signal box at the western were commissioned on 3rd March 1923 (though still with a mechanical type frame).

On 1st March 1910 Mill Hill Park was renamed Acton Town. Just before then, on 10th February 1910, a flying junction was opened allowing down Ealing/South Harrow trains to pass across the local tracks to Hounslow. Acton Town was rebuilt with five platform faces serving three roads at around the same time, allowing improved operation of the local services reversing there from the west.

Despite all this expansion, the District was unable to use to the full its newly electrified network west of Hammersmith so long as it was at the mercy of the L&SWR on the double track viaduct section between Studland Road and Turnham Green. It had sought to duplicate the line in its 1902 Bill, but the L&SWR opposed this, conceding instead some greater operating flexibility and giving the District control over the fares charged at the stations on this section. Nevertheless, growing traffic on the District's proliferating western branches created mounting inconvenience west of Hammersmith and their 1910 Act authorized 4-tracking of the L&SWR viaduct.

Much of the widening took place on the north side of the viaduct and the work was fairly difficult. Ravenscourt Park and Turnham Green were rebuilt with island platforms serving both pairs of lines, but a new station (Stamford Brook, opened 1st February 1912) was built in similar style but with platforms only on the southern pair. The extra lines were opened fully on 3rd November 1911, the District operating the southern pair of tracks, which they electrified and equipped with automatic signals, and the L&SWR using the northern pair; the physical junction at Studland Road was abolished. The L&SWR tracks dived below the District's Acton line tracks west of Turnham Green to join new connecting lines from the District to Richmond. From 11th December 1911 a radically improved District timetable offered many more non-stop trains.

It must have been a little frustrating for the L&SWR to see just how short-lived their investment in 4-tracking proved to be; their service on the northern pair of its expensively widened tracks lasted around five years, after which they lay derelict for nearly 15 years more. Even as the widening was taking place, the GWR steam shuttle from Ladbroke Grove to Richmond ceased; it last operated on 31st December 1910 as the traffic pulled away to the competition, especially the electrified District Railway and LUT trams. When the Metropolitan finally took effective control of the Hammersmith & City line from 1st January 1913, it negotiated with the L&SWR about reusing its running powers to Richmond, including electrification from Hammersmith to Turnham Green. Agreement was nearly secured by summer 1914, but events were to take a different course.

The remote Rayners Lane station looking east. Prior to the arrival of Piccadilly Line trains and surburbia, the station was served only by occasional Met and District trains. Tickets were sold in the hut on the bridge.

The Central London Railway, already extending towards Ealing in an alliance with the Great Western, also wanted to reach Richmond and beyond. The scheme was originally promoted in 1912 while the CLR was independently controlled, but the company was taken over by the UERL from 1st January 1913 resulting in the ideas for extension beyond Richmond being dropped. The CLR Act of 15th August 1913 gave them powers to tunnel via Goldhawk Road, from Shepherd's Bush to east of Gunnersbury, with running powers over the L&SWR from Gunnersbury to Richmond. The LER had equally been considering western extension in that direction and had been mindful of the greater capacity now available west of Hammersmith, the spare LER capacity still available east of Hammersmith and the mounting number of people needlessly changing there. It therefore followed a parallel process to the CLR with its own Act of 15th August authorizing a Piccadilly Line extension from Hammersmith to Richmond, including electrification of the L&SWR viaduct tracks. The latter move would have been much cheaper than the Central London link, though arguably less useful in that it duplicated the District for a considerable distance.

Although the L&SWR had contemplated electrification of its London suburban lines for several years, it was the CLR proposal to go to Richmond and beyond which finally provoked the L&SWR into action on its own behalf. L&SWR passenger traffic in London had fallen by 1,250,000 in the six months to early 1913, attracted to competitors; lines to Richmond and Wimbledon already had electric District trains and clearly the threat of further incursions was not good news. Electrification of L&SWR suburban routes was then announced, using a single low voltage power rail with return current through the running rails. This system could be adapted to accommodate the District's 4-rail pick-up trains or the CLR's 3-rail central-conductor trains, but it would be next to impossible to devise an arrangement where all three could operate on the same track.

The L&SWR had electrified to Richmond by 1915 from the Waterloo direction, and was to give consideration to electrification of the Hammersmith route for its own trains. However, the circuitous L&SWR services had succumbed to more direct competition: electric trams were doing as much damage as the Piccadilly and improved District services were doing. Even without electrifying the Kensington to Turnham Green section, the L&SWR was already obtaining some benefit from the income earned from the buoyant District services, and any others it could encourage of a non-competitive nature. A half-hearted residual steam service was briefly continued by the L&SWR until it fizzled out completely.

The First World War interrupted the intriguing prospect of two UERL tubes and the Metropolitan vying to be the first to get to Richmond. The UERL took the opportunity to buy out the Metropolitan interest, giving compensation in return for an agreement not to exercise running powers. Tracks were severed from the Metropolitan at Hammersmith in November 1914 and removed on 7th May 1916. A month later, on 3rd June 1916, the last L&SWR steam trains ran via Hammersmith, wartime economies being the excuse. As a result, rust and weeds populated the northern pair of the just-widened tracks rather than swift electric trains.

After the First World War an LER extension beyond Hammersmith, or a CLR extension south-west of Shepherd's Bush, remained a continuing aspiration of the UERL. Ownership of the whole line between Addison Road, Studland Road junction and Richmond passed from the L&SWR to the Southern Railway (the 'Southern') in

1923, which company staffed the intermediate stations to Richmond, including Ravenscourt Park, Stamford Brook and Turnham Green, served exclusively by District trains.

It seemed initially to be the Central London Railway which was favoured to use these tracks. In 1920 powers were obtained for a link connecting the Central at Shepherd's Bush with the L&SWR line just west of its disused Shepherd's Bush station, this time much shorter than the line authorized in 1913 – and far cheaper. Financially, the link fell foul of prevailing revenue difficulties; although the fares basis was changing, the fear of mounting pirate bus competition on the UERL's overall revenue was real enough and government help in restricting this was sought (though this did not emerge until 1924). Prospects brightened briefly as the link featured as one of a range of schemes placed before the Government in 1921 for guaranteed funding under the Trade Facilities Act. However, the money authorized fell just short of that requested, schemes such as the Edgware extension of the Hampstead Line took priority and the Central scheme fell into abeyance. In the following years doubts were expressed about the Central's ability to handle additional traffic from Richmond, especially as its Ealing traffic was developing, and it was realized that the busy in-town stations were inadequate for the expanding business. Although the powers for extension were renewed in 1924, authorized capital was diverted to modernization of the busy stations at Shepherd's Bush, along the Oxford Street axis, and in the City in preference to adventures elsewhere.

In 1922 the Underground's chairman (Lord Ashfield) had stated publicly that he desired to serve Richmond, either through the medium of the Central London or the Piccadilly: with the Central London proposal in increasing difficulty, attention returned to the Piccadilly Line where traffic was still at less than maximum capacity and where extension beckoned at each end. But the pressures were not immediately overwhelming. The 1914 powers for an LER extension westwards from Hammersmith were renewed in 1926, but this time additional authority was obtained for extension of four-tracking from Turnham Green to a point just west of Acton Town. By now housing developments in Ealing and beyond were becoming just as much a priority as improved services to Richmond.

An agreement was concluded with the Southern on 10th June 1926 which gave practical control of the stations, signalling and tracks between Studland Road and Turnham Green to the District and LER, though the Southern remained responsible for the viaduct, bridges and earthworks, and for the remainder of the branch from Gunnersbury to Richmond itself. Running powers to Richmond were extended to the LER as well as the District while the Southern could run occasional and special trains (including goods) over their viaduct section. By this time the shareholders had been advised of the desire for parallel fast and slow services on the 4-track section, though it is not stated how this would be done.

Underground capital expenditure between 1926 and 1928 continued to be focused on consolidation of the existing railway, notably station and rolling stock modernization; planning of the future western extension was low key, but was an emerging priority. Since the early 1920s it had become evident that capacity improvements towards Acton and beyond were not only necessary but essential. For example, residential growth of Heston & Isleworth Urban District (which included Hounslow) had risen by only 3,500 in the ten years from 1911 to 1921, but the following 10-year increase looked as though it was getting on for six times that. This traffic increase had been slow in coming; since opening, the Hounslow line had been a somewhat sleepy affair, and although electrification had caused a mild stirring the unattractive services had not been very stimulating. The South Harrow line was worse; not only was housing sparse but competing services ate into the little traffic that existed. There was little incentive for the Metropolitan's Uxbridge line traffic to divert to the District's moth-eaten shuttle; South Harrow and Sudbury competed with Metropolitan and LNER services, Alperton with the London, Midland & Scottish, and Park Royal and North Ealing with the Great Western.

In the morning rush hour of 1922 some 32 trains served the western branches, 19 of which ran to Earl's Court and eastwards. Ealing and Richmond enjoyed all through trains, though Richmond had only five trains compared with Ealing's nine. Hounslow had four through trains compared with South Harrow's singular offering. The majority of the service from South Harrow and Hounslow comprised a motley collection of 2, 3 or 4–car trains shuttling variously to Ealing Common, Acton Town or South Acton.

In the 1925 timetable there were 30 trains on the western branches in the peak hour, 20 going beyond Hammersmith. Hounslow services had been improved by an additional through path and diversion of paths from the Ealing service. Two additional shuttles had appeared on the South Harrow line, but there was still only one through train. (It might be noted that for many years this train ran as an express train, missing out ten or so stations between South Harrow and South Kensington. In 1925 it was run by eight cars of the latest 'F' stock of 1920/1 origin, in stark contrast to the remainder of the service.) Richmond still had a dismal five trains in the peak. The 1930 service shows further through paths have been squeezed into the timetable, with virtually no more capacity available. Off-peak District Railway trains from central London only served Wimbledon, Richmond and Ealing Broadway. Connecting shuttles ran from Acton Town to Northfields and Hounslow, and from South Acton to South Harrow and (half-hourly) Uxbridge.

Boston Manor station looking east immediately prior to work on the Piccadilly extension beginning. The new depot at Northfields was to be built immediately ahead with access tracks behind the right-hand fence. Boston Manor had more substantial buildings than some stations, and platform structures were largely retained when the station was rebuilt.

The solution to these mounting constraints was the proposal to introduce fast and slow services on separate pairs of tracks between Hammersmith and Acton Town, considerably increasing capacity and speeding up services. As implemented, the Piccadilly services ran on the inner pair of tracks offering the fast service, while the District served the outer pair (the first example on the Underground of this method of working). Exactly how this emerged is not wholly clear, nor was the proposed split of services to the western branches, though the principles had been arrived at by 1929. At this stage the running of Piccadilly trains to Richmond had certainly not been ruled out. In the interim some trains, it was stated, would terminate at Turnham Green. The decision that it would be the Piccadilly trains to run the fast service rather than the larger, more comfortable District trains, was to have repercussions over the next 40 years when the service to London Airport was being considered.

Acton Town in 1930 had three roads served by two island platforms. This view looks west showing the westbound road (left) and centre road (right). The centre track is in approximately the same position as today's eastbound Piccadilly Line.

By using the Piccadilly to mop up the increasing demand on the Hounslow and South Harrow lines it freed up District resources, allowing comprehensive re-arrangement of services to all their western branches. The District's services were to be concentrated on the Ealing, Hounslow, Richmond and Wimbledon outlets – with truncated shuttles from South Acton to Acton Town and from South Harrow to Uxbridge (almost entirely on Metropolitan Railway track). Nevertheless, even as late as October 1930, it was proposed to run a few through District trains to South Harrow in rush hours. It was, in the event, several years before service patterns settled down in reaction to frantic 1930s house-building. By 1929 it was intended to extend quadrupling of the line to Northfields (to be reconstructed east of Northfield Avenue, making room for a new depot to the west); this would allow fast trains to continue at least that far. On the new four-track section, Piccadilly trains were to stop only at Hammersmith, Turnham Green, Acton Town (junction for South Harrow) and Northfields, while the District would continue to provide an all-stations service (with limited non-stopping). It was envisaged there would initially be a 2-minute fast Piccadilly service to Acton Town, where one in three trains would turn, leaving a 6-minute Piccadilly service on each of the two branches (augmented by the District). Although provisions for a reversing point at Turnham Green and a link towards Richmond were allowed for, no physical facilities for these were built, though even today the physical arrangements would not rule out such provisions.

Acton Town reconstruction on 30th December 1931, looking west. Work has just begun on reconstructing the northern island platform and building the South Acton bay.

Left This view of the southern Piccadilly platform at Hammersmith shows station reconstruction works having just begun, with southern 'arrival' platform out of use and part demolished to allow a temporary eastbound District platform to be built. This view is taken from a similar position to the picture on page 21.

Below Hammersmith station during reconstruction in June 1931. The old District westbound island is on the right, and the old eastbound track and platform (demolished) is in the centre. The District eastbound line is on a temporary alignment on the curved track on the left. This platform has been built on part of the old Piccadilly Line station and the far end will form today's eastbound Piccadilly Line. While this part of the works was in hand, Piccadilly trains reversed in one platform on the extreme left. The right-hand island was subsequently widened to a point near the disused track in the middle, today's westbound Piccadilly Line. The new signal box, visible on the right parapet wall, has already been commissioned.

A necessary adjunct to increasing capacity on the Hounslow line was the elimination of the final single-track section of the District west of Heston-Hounslow, already forcing some trains to reverse there in preference to the Barracks. But first it is necessary to mention the comprehensive renaming of the various stations in the area: from 1st December 1925 Hounslow Barracks had become Hounslow West, Heston-Hounslow had become Hounslow Central, and Hounslow Town was renamed Hounslow East, their current names. The line between Hounslow Central and Hounslow West was doubled from 27th November 1926, and a new three platform layout at the latter station was brought into use from 11th December, with new signal box (though the original single platform, the southernmost of the three, was temporarily decommissioned until 27th March 1927 for rebuilding). The old station building was retained.

Financing modernization and extension of the Piccadilly became practicable following the Government's Development (Loans Guarantees and Grants) Act in 1929, one of the measures designed to reduce unemployment. After the acquisition of further construction powers in 1930, work on the western extension began in 1931. One of the more difficult tasks was the need to alter track and signalling between West Kensington and Hammersmith to suit a west/west/east/east pattern (from two pairs of east/west flows) while two operational railways were running a full service; the Piccadilly's depot link to Lillie Bridge also had to be maintained. At Hammersmith the District Railway had three platforms serving three tracks, while the Piccadilly had four platforms serving two tracks; all this had to be replaced by an entirely new station of four platforms (two islands) serving four tracks. From December 1930 the work of reconstruction began, with frequent temporary arrangements in force, including an extended period when the entire Piccadilly Line service of 24 trains per hour had only a single track in which to reverse.

Between Hammersmith and the junction with the Southern at Studland Road it was necessary to excavate a second covered way. This emerged at a point where the viaduct swung west, adjacent to the District Line tracks, and there was just room to squeeze one of the new tracks between them. What was to become the new District eastbound line had to be built just north of the viaduct until all the lines ran at the same level. This meant piercing the structure on the curve and the loss of five arches. Bearing in mind that at this point the Southern's line and viaduct was disused, and that the remaining track was being lifted, it seems perverse that the right of way be replaced by a concrete bridge. Nevertheless it stands today (a derelict eyesore), unlike the rest of the route to Olympia which is almost entirely built over.

At Stamford Brook there had only been an island platform on the southernmost pair of lines, used exclusively by District trains. In future these would be the westbound District and Piccadilly tracks, so a new eastbound District platform had to be built alongside the northernmost track (formerly L&SWR to Kensington [Addison Road]). No platform was needed for the non-stop Piccadilly trains, so there exists today on the Piccadilly Line tracks only an unserved westbound platform.

Revised connections were installed east and west of Turnham Green with the Richmond line, including two eastbound goods loops for coal trains to West Kensington and Kensington High Street. The required spoil for this and other nearby embankment works came largely from the excavations for Northfields depot. The northern pair of tracks was projected westwards through Chiswick Park to Acton Town, requiring Chiswick Park station to be completely rebuilt. At Acton Town major reconstruction was required to convert the former three-track (with four platform faces) layout, to a five-track layout, one of which was reserved for a truncated and isolated South Acton shuttle service. The four-tracking continued west to Northfields where a new, and resited, station was built, replacing the structure provided in 1908.

This brought Northfields station significantly closer to South Ealing, whose closure was considered. Northfields was given a secondary entrance at the eastern end of its platforms, a long gallery linking the platforms with Weymouth Avenue, only 200 yards from South Ealing station entrance and less than 70 yards from the western end of South Ealing's platforms. Closure was dependent on two main factors: the opening of another station at Ascott Avenue, in the long stretch between Acton Town and South Ealing, and maintenance of an interchange with local buses, which Weymouth Avenue could not immediately offer. In the event, no buses were to serve Ascott Avenue either, and while some provision was made for a new station there further works were never carried out. South Ealing's eastbound platform was given a contemporary awning and shelter in 1936 but continuing indecision resulted in it retaining the 'temporary' wooden station ticket hall which had been erected while the widening work proceeded – it survived until 1989 when a pleasant modern station building and short westbound shelter were erected – it was the Weymouth Avenue entrance at Northfields which was not to survive, being closed after traffic on 3rd May 1942, the concrete support structure remaining an intriguing site today.

Northfields station was reconstructed as a 4-track station east of Northfield Avenue and opened in 1932. The walkways nearest the camera led to the short-lived Weymouth Avenue exit.

Hammersmith soon after the extension to South Harrow, with reconstruction almost complete and passengers squeezing past an electrician on a trestle to board a four-car Piccadilly Line train with a control trailer in the lead. These four-car trains had only one driving motor car.

Interior of ticket hall, Northfields, around the time of opening. Every encouragement is given to using the automatic ticket machines.

The majority of the tracks west of Barons Court were resignalled as part of the extension work. New signal boxes were built at Hammersmith, Acton Town and Northfields, with signal cabins elsewhere adapted as necessary. Generally, two-aspect signalling was installed where the new boxes were located, but elsewhere a curious mixture of coloured light and electro-pneumatic semaphore signals emerged, the latter being used extensively on the 4-track section. On the South Harrow branch the pioneering automatic signalling with semaphore arms was replaced by new coloured light signalling (commissioned between October and December 1932), but semaphores were retained at North Ealing and South Harrow for some years more. At the latter station a new crossover was installed to enable trains to reverse west to east in either platform, and five new stabling sidings were laid at the eastern end on land used many years earlier for the car sheds for the District's first electric stock. Between the stabling sidings and the eastbound line, a 'traffic' siding was added to facilitate turning around the shuttle service to and from Uxbridge.

Power supplies also needed considerable uprating. A new substation and control room was built at Alperton, and this controlled further new substations at Sudbury Hill, North Ealing and Northfields. New substations also opened at Barons Court and Chiswick Park, the latter remotely controlling the existing District substation at Ravenscourt Park. The existing substations at Hounslow East and Acton Town were retained, but that at Sudbury Town closed. Power was obtained from Lots Road, but an emergency supply from the Metropolitan Railway was available to the substations controlled by Alperton. Substations were subsequently added at Rayners Lane, Eastcote and Uxbridge, supplementing the Metropolitan Railway's at Ickenham.

The western extensions crept into use gradually. The first public indication was a notice that from 8th February 1932 certain local trains to Hounslow and South Harrow would no longer carry first-class accommodation, which the District Railway had provided since opening; this necessarily resulted from infiltration of Piccadilly tube stock onto the District's shuttle services. The shuttles terminated at Acton Town from 14th February, the continuation to South Acton thereafter being served by an independent District shuttle using dedicated District single cars until closure in 1959. Two weeks later first-class accommodation was abandoned completely between Ealing Common and South Harrow.

Experimental running of empty Piccadilly Line trains west of Hammersmith began on 27th June 1932. On 4th July the whole of the District service between Acton Town and South Harrow was withdrawn and replaced by through Piccadilly Line trains, one in three being extended westwards beyond Hammersmith. As part of these works a new depot was brought into use just west of the new station at Northfields. This then had space for a total of 304 cars and included a 19-road car shed and 2-track lifting shop. Temporary access to the depot was available from 29th March 1931 from a point just west of the old station, although the depot was not fully electrified until 29th February 1932. It came into service from 4th July 1932 when some District trains stabled there (probably to make space at Ealing Common for the Piccadilly Line trains needed to operate the South Harrow service). Permanent access to Northfields depot, together with a new 71-lever signal box, was available from 4th September 1932. When the Piccadilly reached Northfields, the new depot then housed Piccadilly trains, some 13 of them stabling there (there were still eight Piccadilly trains stabling at Ealing Common, but the opportunity was taken to cut down those kept at Lillie Bridge to just seven trains and the Aldwych cars).

The Underground Group had wanted in 1930 to send Piccadilly trains to Rayners Lane to connect into Metropolitan Railway services for stations beyond. However, satisfactory terms could not be agreed between the companies, with the result that services beyond South Harrow had to remain as defined in the Metropolitan's 1899 takeover of the Harrow & Uxbridge Railway. From 4th July Piccadilly trains connected at South Harrow (rather inconveniently) with a District shuttle westwards to Uxbridge.

The situation changed substantially on 1st July 1933 when the District Railway, the LER and Metropolitan Railway became part of a new public corporation, the London Passenger Transport Board (LPTB). The LPTB concluded that the public interest was better served by working Piccadilly Line trains beyond South Harrow. In contrast to earlier suggestions that services should terminate at an improved Rayners Lane interchange station, it was now felt that the rapidly developing suburbs demanded through trains all the way to Uxbridge. The immediate requirement was an adjustment of Metropolitan Line platform heights to suit both tube and surface stock. The necessary alterations were put in hand, and a through Piccadilly service to Uxbridge replaced the District's South Harrow–Uxbridge service from 23rd October 1933, though many Piccadilly trains still turned west to east at South Harrow.

This further highlighted the unsatisfactory arrangements at South Harrow, where reversing trains could delay the through services in peak periods. It therefore remained a desirable objective to project these trains to an improved interchange at Rayners Lane, requiring new signalling and a western reversing siding. The new track layout was completed in 1935. Some peak hour trains were extended from South Harrow to Rayners Lane in May 1936. Regular reversing was introduced at Rayners Lane on Sundays from October 1937, and all week from October 1943.

Four-tracking was ready from Acton Town to Northfields on 18th December 1932, and from 9th January 1933 additional Piccadilly Line trains were projected beyond Hammersmith, calling only at Acton Town and Northfields (the temporary terminus). From 13th March nearly all Piccadilly trains were projected beyond Hammersmith, improving services to South Harrow and Northfields, and allowing Piccadilly trains to be extended to Hounslow West. This was accompanied by a reduction in through District peak services from central London to Hounslow.

Off-peak services on the Hounslow branch were a little eccentric. The through Piccadilly Line trains were straightforward enough, and as in the peak hours failed to call at South Ealing which was still regarded as a District Line station (like Ravenscourt Park); public timetables instructed passengers for South Ealing to catch a District Line train. The District had previously run only a shuttle service to Acton Town during the off-peak and there was evidently an attempt to continue the perception of such a service. Between peaks, 2-car sets of Piccadilly stock operated, shown meticulously in the working timetables as District trains and ignored entirely in most passenger timetables (though very early and late each day there were indeed District shuttles continuing to comprise District stock). This unhelpful arrangement continued until 29th April 1935 when an enhanced off-peak Piccadilly service from central London was substituted – resulting in all off-peak trains having to call at South Ealing (peak trains followed from May 1942, resulting from closure of Northfields, Weymouth Avenue entrance). At no point after the introduction of Piccadilly trains did District through trains to South Harrow operate, marking a departure from the earlier plans.

South Harrow facing west on 4th July 1932, the first day of Piccadilly through services. The station had not altered much since opening in 1903; the main station building is on the right and the westbound platform (with short train just visible) was reached by a subway.

Left Uxbridge shortly after arrival of Piccadilly trains in 1934. A short train waits in the main platform with the station building behind.

As with the earlier reconstructions, Park Royal received a temporary station building until a new surface structure was eventually built. The authorities seem to have been keen to avoid giving the impression that this hut might have been the new station itself. It was in use from July 1931 until the end of February 1936.

At Sudbury Hill a temporary station with some features reminiscent of Charles Holden architecture was erected. The former District Railway station is in course of demolition on the right of the picture to make way for the new station.

For the passenger, the new through train services were matched by an unprecedented orgy of station reconstruction. The Underground Group's consulting architects, the Adams, Holden & Pearson practice, visited continental Europe in 1930 and confirmed ideas for further improvements to station designs beyond those attempted in the mid-1920s with the Morden tube extension. They were commissioned to design a reconstruction of Sudbury Town as a prototype design; it was completed on 19th July 1931. The result was considered successful and further station reconstruction by them was spread over six years.

Passengers using the Piccadilly's western extensions saw Hounslow West (1931), Osterley (1934), Northfields (1933), Sudbury Hill (1932), Alperton (1932), Park Royal (1931–36), Ealing Common (1931), Acton Town (1932), and Hammersmith (1932) all totally rebuilt. South Harrow was almost entirely rebuilt, with the platforms shifted westwards by around 200 feet right up to Northolt Road bridge, the new ticket hall coming into use on 5th July 1935; the original station building off South Hill Avenue, less canopies and awning, survives as staff accommodation. Hammersmith retained only its 1906 facade onto the Broadway, but a new one was built facing Queen Caroline Street (though a modern development has swept all this away). Boston Manor station was rebuilt (1934) at ticket hall level, and Stamford Brook gained a new eastbound platform in modern style. The stations are deemed to have architectural merit even now, as Sudbury Town gained Grade II listing in 1971 and others followed; the inability to heat these vast and sometimes draughty structures in winter is perhaps not part of the criteria for listing. Only North Ealing retains the features of an original District Railway suburban station.

Park Royal received a modern station building several years after the Piccadilly Line took over the branch.

The old Park Royal and Osterley stations were closed, replaced by new 'Holden' stations on sites adjoining new arterial roads. Park Royal & Twyford Abbey was largely demolished after a temporary replacement opened on Western Avenue on 6th July 1931, the permanent new station building opening on 1st March 1936. The former Osterley & Spring Grove booking office in Thornbury Road, closed after 24th March 1934, is now a bookshop; some thought was given to providing a footpath to the new station but the cost was not felt justified.

Later, Rayners Lane (1938), Eastcote (1939), Ruislip Manor (1938) and Uxbridge (1938) stations were also rebuilt to the latest architectural standards, though it is perhaps regrettable that the 'round-the-corner' interchange traffic at Rayners Lane was not better catered for by provision of an island platform – two long staircases have to be negotiated. At Uxbridge the station was moved considerably closer to the town centre, under powers in the 1936 LPTB Act, and a new three-track (four-platform) structure replaced a two-platform steam age affair on 4th December 1938; as part of this work, rolling stock sidings were added near the old station (though they were not completed until 1942).

At Hammersmith, Acton Town, Ealing Common, along the Hounslow branch and between Rayners Lane and Uxbridge, all platforms were altered to 'compromise' height, half way between the car floor levels of tube and surface stock, giving a rather high step up into District and Metropolitan Line trains. This seems also to have been attempted between North Ealing and South Harrow, but with no District trains actually operating, the tracks have been raised slightly to minimize the step into the Piccadilly trains.

Sudbury Town was regarded as a prototype of the bold new designs proposed for the Piccadilly extensions. A temporary entrance was built (at far left) while the main building was erected.

Reconstruction at platform level was equally comprehensive and it is to be noted the station remained open throughout reconstruction. The station was regarded as a good interchange with the Metropolitan Electric Trams, referred to on the old signboards but not on their replacements.

Sudbury Town – the finished result, 1932.

By way of contrast, Holborn was typical of the congested central London stations struggling to cope with rising traffic. This view is taken from the High Holborn entrance in August 1930 (shortly before the station was rebuilt); electrically operated ticket machines and a 1920s Passimeter ticket office have been installed in front of the old ticket office, the lifts being behind it. Imminent reconstruction was to sweep away this clutter, with four new escalators leading down to the lower station (see next chapter).

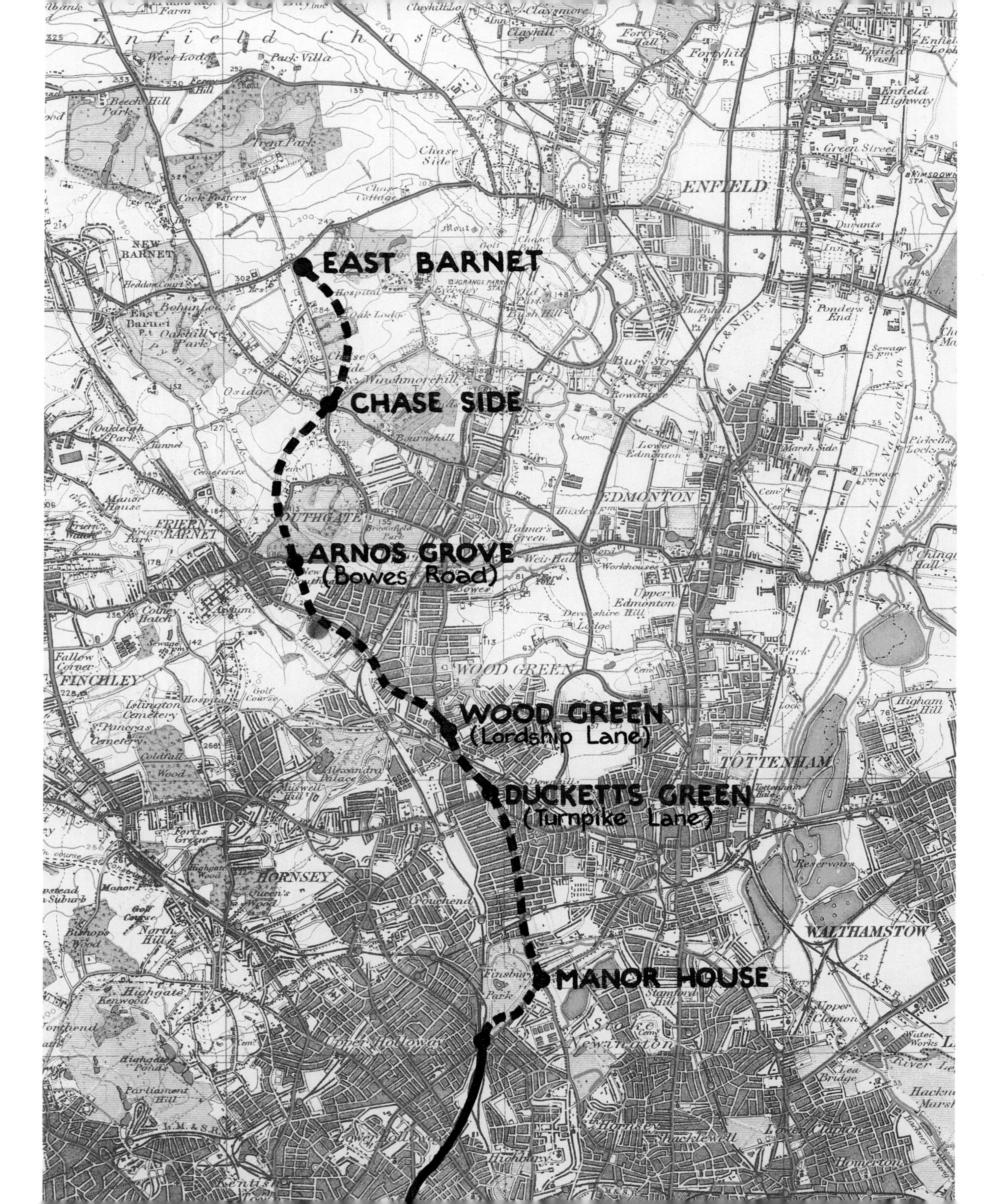
EAST BARNET
CHASE SIDE
ARNOS GROVE
(Bowes Road)
WOOD GREEN
(Lordship Lane)
DUCKETTS GREEN
(Turnpike Lane)
MANOR HOUSE

EXPANSION IN THE NORTH AND CENTRAL AREA MODERNIZATION

The western extensions of the Piccadilly represented only half the line's thrust into the newly developing suburbs. An extension northwards from Finsbury Park, envisaged as an integral part of the original Great Northern & Strand project, remained a pressing requirement – though still blocked by the absolute undertaking agreed between Yerkes and the Great Northern Railway in 1901. Finsbury Park was the northern terminus of both the Piccadilly Line and the Great Northern & City Railway, and was an extremely busy place. Not only was there a substantial exchange of traffic with the main line railway, itself overcrowded and using out-of-date suburban trains, but there was also massive interchange with both trams and buses, with no purpose-built facilities, reflecting the geographical fact of the London suburbs in North London which already extended beyond Tottenham and Palmers Green. The situation was regarded as intolerable by many observers.

The Great Northern Railway periodically reviewed electrification of the main line out of King's Cross but could not afford it even without the disadvantage of competing tubes. As matters grew worse the attitude of the GNR (and, after 1923, its successor, the London & North Eastern Railway) towards any tube extension was widely considered unreasonable. The GNR vetoed a 1920 proposal by the LER to extend the Piccadilly Line northwards.

In 1925 the London & North Eastern Railway conceded that it could not afford electrification, and reluctantly acknowledged that if it were not itself able to improve travelling facilities then it could not reasonably withhold consent to a tube extension. An Inquiry held by the London & Home Counties Traffic Advisory Committee in October 1925 came to the conclusion that an extension was warranted, and the Underground Group made preparatory moves towards meeting the need. Various districts had applied pressure for the tube to serve their own territory, but it could not serve all of them directly. The Committee supported an extension to Manor House, and an interchange station there with trams and buses; the tube company was advised also to explore the possibility of extension to Wood Green or Southgate. The interchange at Manor House would be 'invaluable' for 'the districts of Tottenham, Edmonton, and the Eastern part of Enfield' who 'would continue to rely largely upon the tramway services'.

Unfortunately the Underground Group was not in a much better position than the LNER to pay for the high cost of new capital works, but the passing in 1929 of the Development (Loan Guarantees and Grants) Act at last made possible, as with the western extensions, the financing of a substantial northward projection. The LER successfully sought powers in 1930, despite continued LNER opposition and promises of main line electrification if the tube scheme were dropped. In October 1930 the overall costs of the Piccadilly Line extensions were estimated as £7.7 million before interest, comprising £4.4 million and £2.3 million respectively for the northern and western extensions, and £1 million for rolling stock. Further costs were to be incurred by alterations to the existing Piccadilly Line, including station reconstruction in central London. The overall cost of Underground works (including other schemes) to take advantage of the Development Act was £12.4 million and the Treasury guaranteed interest on nearly £10 million for the following 15 years, by which time the works should have been capable of paying their way. The northern extension was forecast to carry 36 million passengers a year once the open fields beyond Wood Green had high-quality housing, filled with affluent travellers.

The terminus was initially planned to be 6.75 miles from Finsbury Park, in green fields at East Barnet, the need for a large depot requiring the line to continue at least this far out. The depot site first recommended was just south of the proposed East Barnet station and to be above the running line as it dropped into tunnel for about half a mile. This plan changed by November 1929 – at least part of the reason being the operational objection to a 'single-ended' depot. The new site was somewhat larger, to the north of the station, spreading most of the way towards Trent Park. This added a new terminus to the scheme, initially named after the park but soon called Cockfosters.

These aerial photographs along the route of the Northern extension show clearly how rural the part of London beyond Arnos Grove still was.

EAST BARNET

Aerial view of the line at leafy Cockfosters with the depot clearly visible and Enfield West station in the distance by the road bridge.

To the north of Finsbury Park the extension would at last achieve the original intention of the old Great Northern & Strand Railway – to relieve the pressure of suburban traffic on the main line railway – though the exact line of route was somewhat different. Intermediate stations (with their earlier public names prior to opening within the brackets) were to be at Manor House, Turnpike Lane (ex-Ducketts Green), Wood Green (ex-Lordship Lane), Bounds Green (ex-Brownlow Road), Arnos Grove (ex-Bowes Road), and Southgate (ex-Chase Side). East Barnet was hurriedly renamed Enfield West just before opening, then Enfield West (Oakwood) on 3rd May 1934, and finally plain Oakwood on 1st September 1946. A pair of stations had originally been intended for Harringay, at St Anne's Road and Turnpike Lane; the former was deleted to keep average speeds high – a recurring priority for the extension – in

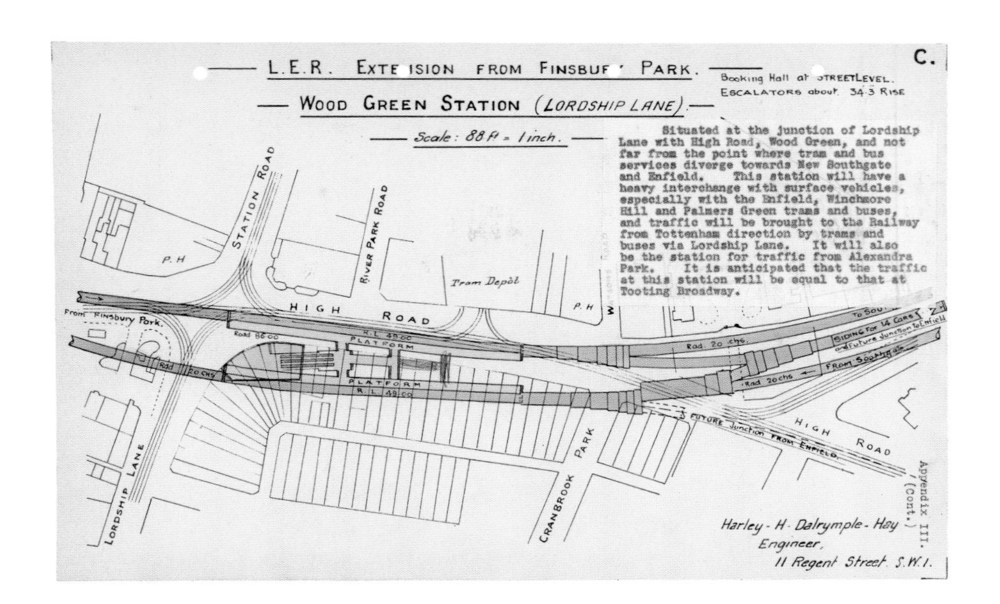

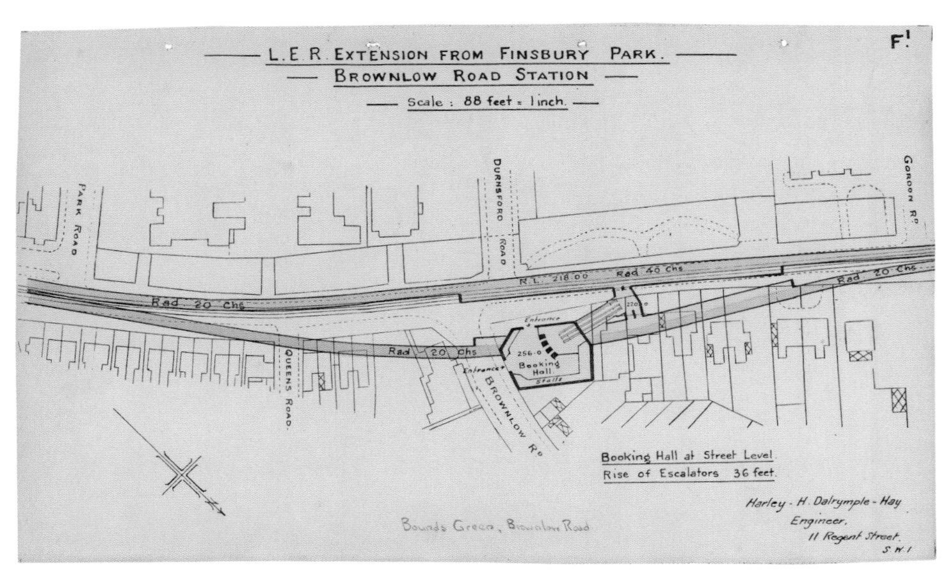

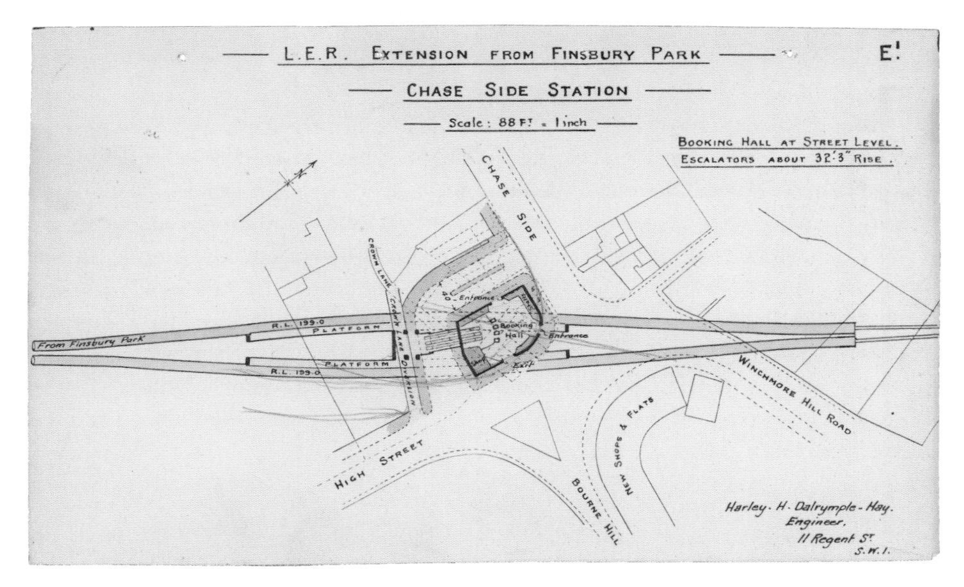

Plans for three of the stations as drawn up in 1929. The layout at Wood Green allowed for a possible future branch to Enfield. Brownlow Road station became Bounds Green, and Chase Side became Southgate.

Chase Side, Southgate, had not changed a great deal since Edwardian days. The new station was built next to the point from which this photograph was taken.

substitution for a proposed third track between Finsbury Park and Wood Green. Inter-available Train-Omnibus-Tram tickets were to be offered instead for passengers to intermediate points. Bounds Green station nearly went the same way, being put back in the scheme between June and September 1929. The station names chosen were by no means geographically accurate. Enfield West station was located on East Barnet Road (now Bramley Road), and whilst three quarters of a mile away from East Barnet village, it was much closer than built-up Enfield (with 'Enfield West' being an invention). Southgate station was near one of Southgate's historical centres. Arnos Grove was in New Southgate. The chosen names inevitably imposed themselves on the soon-to-be-built-up suburbs and provided a measure of exclusiveness, no doubt to the pleasure of the estate agents.

The station site at Southgate, with Chase Side visible on the right. The proposed names on the board were Chase Side, Southgate and Southgate Central.

Southgate nears completion, leaving the small green unspoilt. This astonishingly bold architectural design adopted at a fairly late stage contrasts starkly with the old world surroundings.

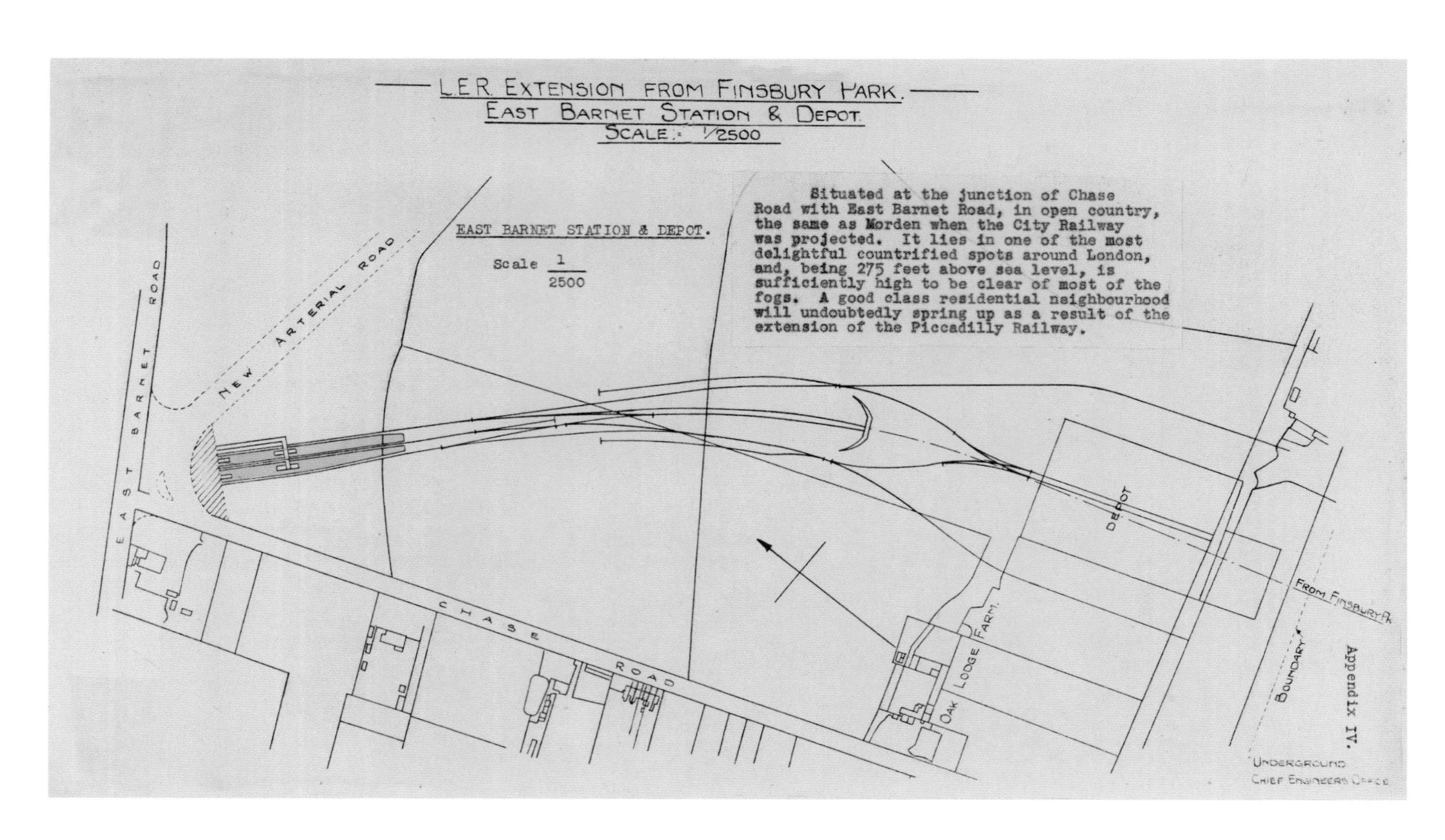

Enfield West was at first intended to be the terminal of the northern extension, with the depot to its south. Operational objections resulted in the depot being relocated to the north of the station and projection of the 3-track terminus to Cockfosters, a simple island being substituted.

The platforms at Enfield West, looking south during October 1932.

The railway at Enfield West was especially remote and the photo on the left, taken on 8th September 1930, is looking towards the future station building. Although the station finally opened as Enfield West, it was not one of the suggested names on the site board.

The station at Wood Green was on the corner of High Road and Lordship Lane and required demolition of existing property. Like most stations on the extension, names were fixed only after a period of public consultation around a small number of suggestions.

All platforms on the extension were at first intended to be 400ft long, enough for 8-car trains (but were only 385ft long as built); at Manor House, Turnpike Lane and Wood Green the platform tunnels were 2ft wider than was normal, in anticipation of heavy traffic. Thought was given to passive provision at Manor House for a branch to Tottenham, or to an eventual parallel extension of the Great Northern & City Line to Manor House in case interchange problems developed underground at Finsbury Park; the GN&CR might then head for Tottenham (an early precursor to the Victoria Line that was built in the 1960s). Reversing sidings were planned at Manor House and Wood Green, the latter layout intended to allow for a future junction with a branch line in the Enfield direction. In the event nothing additional was provided at Manor House and the siding at Wood Green made no provision for any future branch. Stabling sidings and further reversing facilities were provided at Arnos Grove (a reversing siding was all that was originally intended, but the final design included a three-track, four-platform station including a centre reversing platform road). To keep average speeds high, 25 mph or more, and to reduce maintenance, sharp curves were avoided, while at 12ft the tunnel diameter was slightly more generous than on the original line.

Initial planning for the rolling stock ignored developments at the west end of the line (probably because the District Railway would have been expected to pay for those 21 or so trains as they owned the track – the cars would merely be added to the order) and assumed no station at Bounds Green and the closure of seven existing Piccadilly Line stations as part of a drive to improve speeds (these were Gloucester Road, Brompton Road, Down Street, Covent Garden, York Road, Caledonian Road and Gillespie Road). From the 1929 viewpoint, around 26 to 27 trains an hour were to be projected northwards, half turning at Wood Green, and the remainder proceeding to Enfield West, for which 128 extra cars (74 motor, 54 trailers – about 18 trains) were thought needed in addition to the basic fleet of 192 cars. After Bounds Green was reinstated, there were thoughts of alternately skip-stopping that station and Arnos Grove, to maintain the same journey times. However, by October 1930 the main service was then expected to terminate at Arnos Grove until traffic built up, with a shuttle to Cockfosters. It is important to recall that beyond Arnos Grove there was almost no housing at all.

Work on the northern extension began quickly once the Act of Parliament had been obtained. The line was to run in twin tube tunnel from Finsbury Park to Tewkesbury Terrace, north of Bounds Green – the running tunnels were bored rapidly, at the rate of one mile a month. The line then rose to viaduct level having crossed the North Circular Road on a 173ft long steel bridge. Arnos Grove and East Barnet/Enfield West were surface stations, but the intermediate station at Southgate was in a further length of twin tube tunnel. Cockfosters consisted of a three-track terminus, with four platforms, enclosed within a concrete roof.

Signal cabins were built at Cockfosters, Enfield West, Arnos Grove and Wood Green, two-aspect coloured light signals being used throughout. Wood Green signal cabin was unusual in that it could be switched out of service but still provide a facility to reverse trains, instructions being obtained from the train description apparatus with supervision from Arnos Grove cabin – a similar facility allowed Enfield West to control Arnos Grove; this was amongst the first attempts on the Underground to

This diagram shows one of the proposed service patterns prior to the extensions opening. This still shows the intention of reversing part of the service at Turnham Green, running peak Districts to South Harrow (and presumably Uxbridge), and a shuttle only between Cockfosters and Arnos Grove (accounting for the track layout there). Reversing half the service at Wood Green would have been quite a struggle in practice with a 30-train-per-hour service.

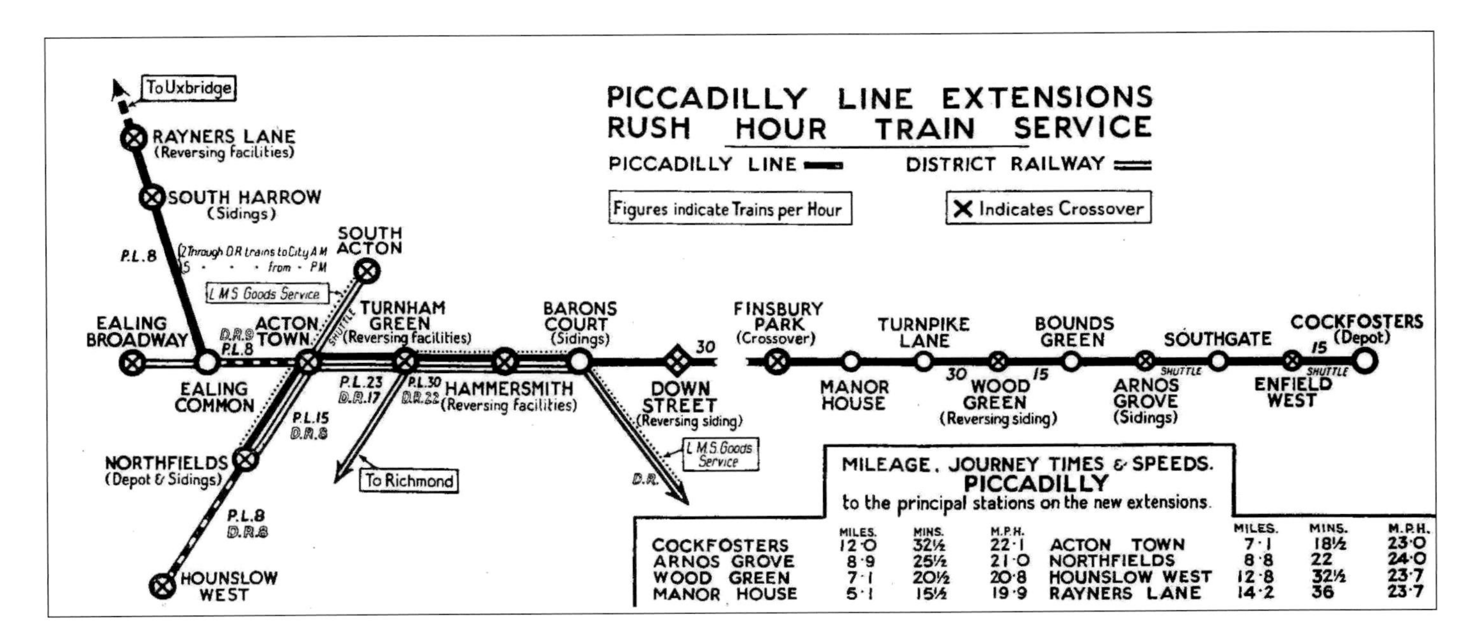

	MILES.	MINS.	M.P.H.		MILES.	MINS.	M.P.H.
COCKFOSTERS	12·0	32½	22·1	ACTON TOWN	7·1	18½	23·0
ARNOS GROVE	8·9	25½	21·0	NORTHFIELDS	8·8	22	24·0
WOOD GREEN	7·1	20½	20·8	HOUNSLOW WEST	12·8	32½	23·7
MANOR HOUSE	5·1	15½	19·9	RAYNERS LANE	14·2	36	23·7

ARNOS GROVE STATION SITE
UNDERGROUND
ARNOS GROVE
STATION SITE
RAILWAY
FROM FINSBURY PARK
ARNOS GROVE STATION SITE

UNDERGROUND
ARNOS GROVE STATION
PICCADILLY 25 MINS
HAMMERSMITH 39 MINS

Work in progress at Arnos Grove, with new housing in the background.

The viaduct across Arnos Park was necessary owing to the sharp drop in levels between Bounds Green and Southgate. This image, taken on 27th April 1932, shows the viaduct complete to parapet level with brickwork nearing completion.

control signalling remotely. Rails were welded in 90ft lengths (double the usual length) to promote quieter running, useful when train speeds were high because of long inter-station distances (peak speeds were up to 50 mph). The electricity supply for the extension was provided by the North Metropolitan Electric Power Supply Company (which was associated with the UERL) and brought in at Wood Green where there was a substation and control room (duplicate lighting supplies came from Lots Road, as on the existing below-ground network). Additional substations were built at Manor House, Wood Green, Arnos Grove, Southgate and Cockfosters, and the existing substation at Holloway Road was re-equipped and linked to the new control room. Plans for a further substation at York Road were not pursued.

Looking south from the tunnel mouth south of Southgate shows the largely unspoilt scene as the land drops sharply away towards Arnos Grove, requiring the line to be carried on viaduct. Tracklaying is shortly to commence.

The site of the terminal platforms at Cockfosters shortly after works commenced.

WOOD GREEN
ARNOS GROVE
SOUTHGATE

Most substations on the northern and western extensions were unmanned and were operated by remote control from a small number of control rooms. This view of the control room at Wood Green shows some of the panels that controlled the substations on the northern extension.

Cockfosters station nearing completion in August 1933.

Architecture on the new works received (as on the Western extensions) painstaking treatment from the Adams, Holden & Pearson practice. The stations reflected the success of Piccadilly Circus, with considerable attention given to finishes and to detail (not all of which proved durable). The surface buildings were spacious and distinctive, being of concrete with considerable brick facings and glazing. Turnpike Lane was, for example, a huge rectangular structure with a brick tower in one corner, but Southgate was a somewhat shallower, drum-like building surmounted by a curious, futuristic finial. Arnos Grove, Southgate and Oakwood (formerly Enfield West) gained Grade II listing in 1971, resulting in some restoration of original station features. Free standing, Passimeters were the norm, with additional wall windows for use in the peaks provided as necessary. At the tunnel stations the escalator shafts were wide enough for three machines, though Bounds Green and Southgate had only two machines astride a staircase. Aside from Turnpike Lane and Southgate, the escalators ran at 165 feet a minute and were then the fastest on the system. There were some intriguing experiments at Manor House with attempts to encourage passengers to step on the escalator three at a time. Posts were used to create three streams and the escalator comb was 'staggered', apparently to create the illusion of three spaces; adverse public comment coupled with evidence of some danger caused a rethink. The result was a 'parabolic' comb with more posts and horizontal arms to separate the flows; this created new and more serious difficulties and, mindful of the unpromising public reaction, the experiments were abandoned.

Left The station building at Enfield West, together with the forecourt designed to make bus interchange easy, sits tranquilly amongst the trees in this remote area; but it wasn't very long before the houses came.

Below Platforms at Enfield West on 22 August 1934. The station had been open only 16 months but there is some evidence of finishes having already deteriorated. The gaps in the current rails on the right are positioned at the points where trains coupled or uncoupled to make it safer for staff. Enfield West sported on canopy supports reproductions of the armorial bearings of Southgate Borough Council, awarded on 15th September 1933, upon its elevation from urban district soon after the station opened. The station was the only one situated in the borough (Southgate itself just being in East Barnet Valley Urban District). The motto reads 'From the acorn, the oak' and recalls the oak forests once covering the area; a red rose recalls that the district was once owned by the Duchy of Lancaster.

ARNOS GROVE STATION
NOW RUNNING
ARNOS GROVE

UNDERGROUND
UNDERGROUND
WOOD GREEN
OPEN
NOW OPEN

Above Turnpike Lane was a major interchange with tram services. It is not perhaps obvious from the photograph that the booking hall was actually below street level.

Above left Arnos Grove exterior soon after opening, but with works not quite complete.

Left Wood Green at the time of opening, and again not quite finished.

Lower escalator landing at Southgate on 24th February 1933 showing effects of reflected lighting.

Opposite Wood Green was one of the stations to have larger diameter tunnels which allowed wider platforms with less curved walls.

Engineering difficulties at Wood Green, a busy interchange for tram services, prevented construction of a sub-surface booking hall with pedestrian subway links as at Manor House and Turnpike Lane. There, special efforts were made to improve interchange conditions (in contrast to the chaos that had existed at Finsbury Park), particularly for road services to those suburbs which had lobbied and failed to attract the tube extension. At Manor House, there was an exit direct from the sub-surface booking hall to tramcar-loading islands in the centre of the road for services to Stamford Hill, Seven Sisters, Tottenham and beyond. A similar exit at Turnpike Lane led to loading islands for trams to Alexandra Palace, Hornsey and Tottenham. Bus forecourts were provided at Turnpike Lane, Southgate and Enfield West, and private car parks at Arnos Grove and Enfield West.

Considerable use was made of floodlighting or concealed lighting, to good effect in enhancing the feeling of spaciousness. An attempt was made to dispel what was described as: 'the feeling of being in a tunnel' by means of lights shining down the walls (both track and platform sides), an effect further enhanced by the non-circular section of the platform tunnels at Manor House, Turnpike Lane and Wood Green, where the finishes were more vertical than usual. Platforms were finished in square tiles and incorporated ventilation ducts with bronze 'art deco' style grilles. Good ventilation was a feature of the extension, and in addition to powerful fans at stations there were intermediate tunnel fans at Finsbury Park (tennis courts), Colina Road and Nightingale Road.

NEXT TRAIN
HOUNSLOW
WAY OUT
WOOD GREEN
ALLOW PASSENGERS TO ALIGHT FIRST PLEASE

Two strikingly designed posters for the same extension.

OPENING OF THE
PICCADILLY
LINE
EXTENSION
FINSBURY
PARK
TO
ARNOS
GROVE
ARNOS
GROVE
BOUNDS
GREEN
WOOD
GREEN
TURNPIKE
LANE
MANOR
HOUSE
FINSBURY
PARK
PICCADILLY
UNDERGROUND
5
NEW STATIONS
FOR NORTH
LONDON
19TH • OPEN
SEPTEMBER
C W BACON

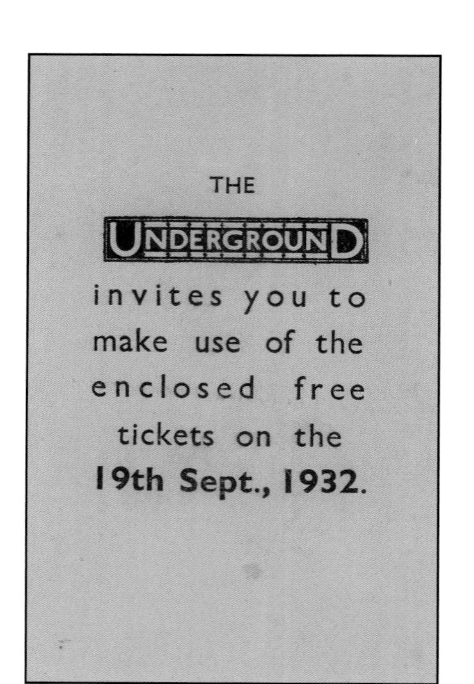

Trains were extended from Finsbury Park to Arnos Grove on 19th September 1932, to Enfield West on 13th March 1933, and Cockfosters at the end of the first month of LPTB ownership, on 31st July 1933. Free tickets for travel on the first days were distributed to local residents. The completion of Cockfosters depot finally allowed the extremely inconvenient depot at Lillie Bridge to be closed down to service trains; in due course the site at Lillie Bridge was adapted to become a central depot for engineers' and materials trains for the whole system.

The early results from the extension were very encouraging, though still not sufficient for the line to pay its way until the area was substantially built up to Cockfosters (which did not happen to the extent anticipated). A total of 25 million passengers had used the line by the end of 1933, by which time interchange traffic with trams and buses at stations north of Finsbury Park had built up to an annualized rate of 11 million passengers, with Manor House and Wood Green each attracting over 3½ million and Turnpike Lane over 2 million.

When all the extensions were open, there were initially 57 of the latest 7-car trains in service, including one spare, plus the 2-car Aldwych train; additional trains were quickly added to the timetable as traffic developed. Initially the bulk of the trains on the northern extension ran at least to Arnos Grove, with roughly one in three projected to Cockfosters (the proposal for an independent shuttle having lapsed). Off peak, 3-car trains were run.

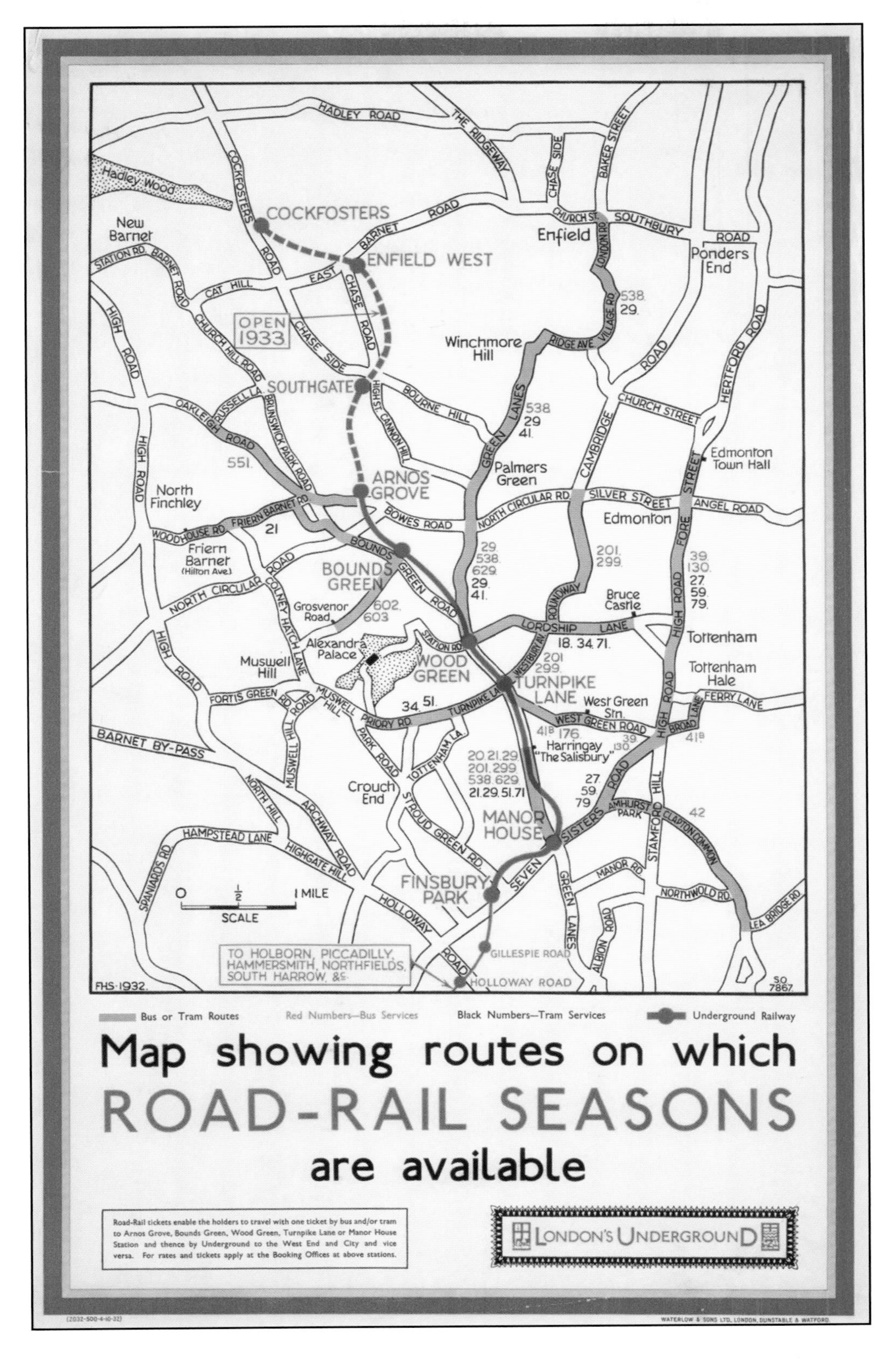

The Underground was extremely anxious to develop traffic along the new extensions and extensive road-rail through tickets were available via connecting bus or tram services, this map showing the local roads along which through bookings were possible. Road-rail seasons remained generally available until 13th October 1967 when they were restricted to existing users. On 18th June 1978 they were withdrawn entirely. 'Suburban bus pass' extensions and, today, travelcards do the same job.

Although the northern extensions opened without ceremony, HRH the Prince of Wales (later Edward VIII) visited the line on 14th February 1933 in order to inspect the all British electrical equipment that was used to equip the works (not something that would be possible on recent extensions). A special book of photographs was presented to him for the occasion.

Although there were some acknowledged 'teething difficulties' it was said at the time that 'this extension represents the best known Underground practice of its type at the present time'. The LER proudly hosted a visit from the Prince of Wales on 14th February 1933 when he travelled by train to Wood Green from Piccadilly Circus (driving the train from Manor House); after due inspection of the facilities there he returned by train to Hyde Park Corner and 'inspected' some 14 staff who had been present on the opening day of the City & South London Railway on 18th December 1890, and opened by the Prince's grandfather, King Edward VII, when he was Prince of Wales.

But the transformation did not end merely by extending the Piccadilly Line beyond recognition. There had been very little modernization in the central area, and the new extensions were expected to impose considerable strain on the line unless it were overhauled. Physical capacity was enhanced partly by resignalling the line and partly by rationalizing the station facilities. As noted earlier, the view was taken that the closure of lightly used inner stations would allow a useful speeding up of services and benefit the majority of passengers. Of the seven stations viewed for possible closure, it was decided to close Brompton Road, Down Street and York Road. The Aldwych branch, which 'serves very little purpose, and does not show an adequate return upon the capital incurred', was also reviewed. A £750,000 extension to Waterloo was mooted in 1929 but not proceeded with: the branch was nevertheless reprieved.

Down Street closed after traffic on 21st May 1932, replaced by a resited Hyde Park Corner station entrance with escalators from 23rd May. Brompton Road station closed on 29th July 1934, replaced the following day by a new western escalator entrance (adjoining Harrods) for the rebuilt Knightsbridge station. Knightsbridge had a second new escalator entrance on the corner of Sloane Street; the old station building was closed, with most of it acquired by the adjacent Basil Hotel. An earlier attempt at closing Brompton Road had been made during the 1926 coal strike but it reopened after questions were asked in Parliament (both Brompton Road and York Road stations were shut for five months). The existing emergency crossover and signal cabin were retained at York Road, which closed without replacement on 17th September 1932, two days before the northern extension opened to Arnos Grove. At Down Street part of the platform area was used as the entrance to a new double-length reversing siding, in service from 30th May 1933, which was built between the running lines and controlled from the signal cabin at Hyde Park Corner.

After the First World War the skip-stopping policy extended westwards from King's Cross to include (at various times of the day) either Covent Garden or Russell Square, Brompton Road and South Kensington, though the latter pairing did not endure. As the Piccadilly extended and central London stations were rebuilt, non-stopping was simplified to pairs of stations north of King's Cross plus combinations of Gloucester Road, Brompton Road (until it was closed), and Covent Garden. For a while (until its closure) York Road was served by two out of three trains which greatly complicated the variations of non-stopping patterns possible; most other stations were missed by alternate trains.

Once the western extensions opened, the non-stopping arrangements became even more complex as additional stations were added to the non-stopping patterns. By 1938 Boston Manor, South Ealing and North Ealing were included in the patterns, and Barons Court had also reappeared. Early during the Second World War non-stopping was no longer scheduled except during rush hours, and patterns were again simplified with only the usual tunnel stations (and Barons Court) being non-stopped. This was the beginning of the end, and non-stopping was finally abandoned in June 1947. Trains that did not call at all stations were marked by an unhelpful 'Non Stop' board carried underneath the destination display, but there were no further clues about which stations the trains were not to call, except for shouted announcements. From about 1932 passengers were assisted by illuminated signs on most platforms which displayed the stations at which each train was not going to call as well as its final destination.

Above Press advertisement (from the *Railway Magazine*, July 1932) announcing the opening of the new ticket hall at Hyde Park Corner.

Left The old Hyde Park Corner station entrance in the 1950s. It remains today as the entrance to a restaurant.

Poster showing the new main entrance to Knightsbridge station and the three stairwell entrances.

KNIGHTSBRIDGE

STATION

RECONSTRUCTED

THREE NEW ENTRANCES
ESCALATORS DIRECT FROM TICKET HALL TO PLATFORMS
SUBWAY ROAD CROSSINGS

ANOTHER DEVELOPMENT OF

Above The installation of escalators at the east end of Knightsbridge required an entirely new below-street ticket hall with entrances from street stairwells and by cutting into part of the Knightsbridge branch of Barclays Bank, shown here in April 1934.

Left The platforms at several stations, including Knightsbridge, were entirely redecorated to accord with the new ticket halls and other facilities, and all traces of the 'Yerkes' era were swept away at these. This station has recently been redecorated in an entirely modern style and these finishes have in turn been swept away.

Dover Street station was rebuilt with escalators and completed on 18th September 1933; it was renamed Green Park. The new westerly entrance further mitigated the closure of Down Street station. At Leicester Square two banks of new escalators led down from a circular ticket hall beneath the road intersection, one bank for the Northern and the other (then the longest in the world) to the Piccadilly. The new station opened on 4th May 1935 (although it had been temporarily opened on 27th April to handle Cup Final traffic) and the lifts were then abandoned. Holborn benefited from major reconstruction and an interchange with the Central London Line which the Piccadilly crossed. In this case it was the nearby Central London station at British Museum which closed, with new interchange platforms provided further east and open from 25th September 1933. Four escalators led to an intermediate level (which served the new Central London Line platforms), and thence three more escalators led to the Piccadilly Line level. Escalator access to the Piccadilly Line had opened on 19th May 1933. Reconstruction of Russell Square and King's Cross stations was deferred owing to a worsening financial situation. Russell Square retains lift access today, but King's Cross tube stations (Piccadilly and Northern Lines) were finally combined and rebuilt with escalators during the 1935–40 New Works Programme, the new joint facilities opening on 18th June 1939. Earl's Court was largely rebuilt at street level in 1937, though the Earl's Court Road 1905/06 facade was, and still is, retained having been given a major refurbishment in 2005.

Leicester Square old station in May 1935 with reconstruction work in hand. Perhaps surprisingly, the original railway name has survived in the glasswork next to the entrance. The line control office was situated on the first floor level of this building.

One of the new station entrances being constructed at Leicester Square, 1933. This entrance is at the corner of Cranbourn Street and Charing Cross Road and is opposite the old station. The new ticket hall is beneath the road intersection itself.

The signalling in the original section of the Piccadilly Line had been subject to a process of continuous improvement since around the First World War, with the moving spectacle signals gradually (but not entirely) superseded by coloured light signals, and the addition of multiple home signals to improve headways. Much of the remaining original signalling was updated in 1931 for higher speed working.

Below The upper escalator flight at the reconstructed Holborn station.
This was, and remains, the only station on the Underground to have four escalators in a single excavated shaft, requiring an extremely large tunnel at substantially greater cost.

At King's Cross in 1927 a physical link was opened between the eastbound Piccadilly Line and the northbound line of the just-reconstructed City & South London Railway to allow rolling stock from that railway and the Hampstead Line to reach a new central overhaul depot at Acton; the connection (still there today) was controlled from a small signal cabin on the C&SLR's platforms (that railway and the Hampstead Line are now the major part of the Northern Line, named as such in 1937).

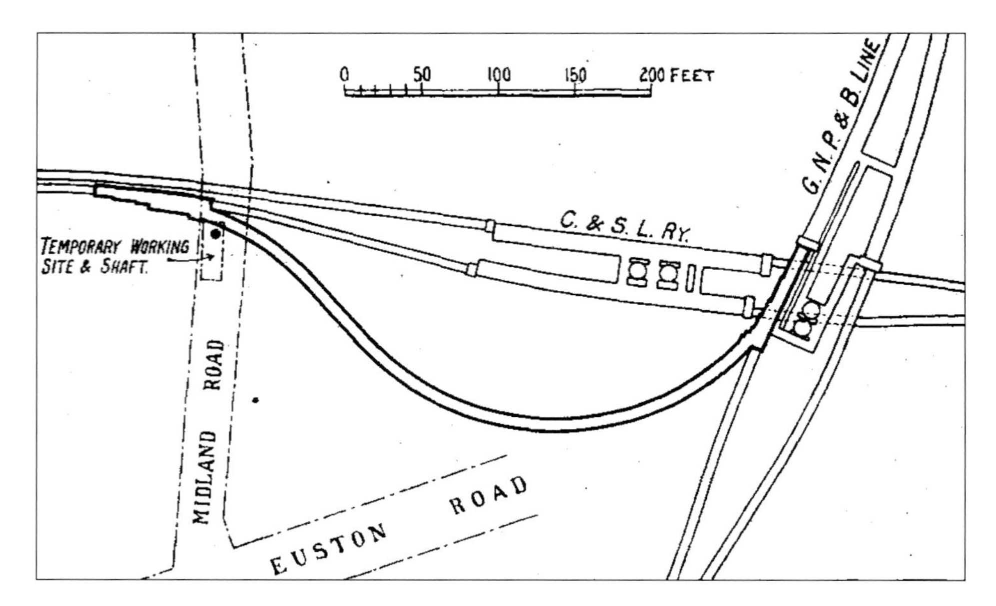

Boarding time at stations was inconveniently slow with only one or two doorways per car and in 1929 it was suggested that a car should be fitted experimentally with three pairs of double doors. Although matters took a different course, in 1930 a 6-car experimental train was ordered from the Union Construction Company at Feltham, and this consisted of two driving motor cars and four trailers. The motor cars were around a foot longer than older stock and included a single-leaf air-operated door at the guard's position; this door could be operated by the guard independently of the passenger doors when he occupied the gangway, but at other times both the door and the gangway were available for passenger use. The trailer cars were about two feet longer than older stock. Two of these included end doors and the other two just had wider double doorways than normal. All the experimental cars required the ends to be slightly tapered to accommodate the loading gauge around curves.

An order for 275 new cars followed, of which there were 145 driving motors (from the Metropolitan-Cammell Carriage, Wagon & Finance Company) and 130 trailers (90 from the Birmingham Railway Carriage & Wagon Company, 40 from the Gloucester Railway Carriage & Wagon Company), at a cost of £1,074,000. £226,000

A motor car of the 1934 stock designed for the Piccadilly extensions. These were the first production cars to have airworked single doors at the trailing end. There were several attempts to apply line branding to rolling stock during this period, but transfers between lines made this feature an operational irritation and it did not endure.

was charged to the District as its share for the western extensions. A transfer of cars between the Piccadilly, Hampstead and Bakerloo Lines also meant that the Piccadilly gained 15 control trailers and lost 15 trailers – the Piccadilly otherwise had enough control trailers already. The new design leant heavily on the experimental train where experience in service favoured the use of trailers with end doors (the distance between door centres on adjacent cars was otherwise considered excessive). Interior design and lighting levels were improved and new weight reducing techniques were employed. Trains were fitted with the then novel electro-pneumatic brake system and 'shunt field' control, which helped to improve overall performance. Total fleet size was now 469 cars – 212 motors (M), 67 control trailers (CT), 188 trailers (T) and the two Aldwych cars. Trains were usually formed into 7-car sets at busy times with a 4-car (M-T-T-M) formation at the west end and a 3-car portion (CT-T-M) at the east. At first the 3-car portion remained in service during Monday-Friday off-peak times but the 4-car sets were used off-peak on Saturdays and on Sundays. In the mid-1930s 4-car off-peak trains became standard.

The previously unplanned extension of Piccadilly trains to Uxbridge in 1933 produced a shortage of rolling stock, a problem redressed by ordering another 26 motor cars from Metropolitan-Cammell (the 1934 stock) for £122,000, speeding up the Hampstead Line fleet with further, consequential, car transfers, and a decision to make the engineering spares 'work harder' for a larger fleet of 509 modern cars plus the two Aldwych cars. The new stock balance was 227 motor cars, 71 control trailers and 211 trailers, which gave 64 7-car trains available for service. It was also intended to order another 6-car train of an experimental new design at a cost of £20,000, as an experimental unit which would work on the Piccadilly Line.

When the bulk of this work was complete, the Piccadilly Line had been transformed within around five years from an antiquated and slow inner suburban tube line to a thoroughly modernized, attractive and relatively fast line reaching out far into the brand new Middlesex suburbs. At the time the distance from Cockfosters to Uxbridge, 31.6 miles, was the longest on the Underground to use electric trains.

Interior of 1931 stock trailer car.

It might be wondered how successful the strategy was of extending the Underground into remote open country at the northern end of the Piccadilly, and of expanding capacity at the western end so much ahead of demand. Although some of the works in and close to the central area were needed physically, they could only be afforded if the overall increase in traffic to the UERL was sufficient to pay the interest on the capital required, even with government guarantees. Extending into the open fields and making lightly used branches more attractive was the only way of generating the new traffic that could ultimately make a whole scheme affordable; merely switching people from tram to train more efficiently, however desirable, did not of itself generate the funds needed. The Development (Loans Guarantees and Grants) Act 1929 allowed the Government to agree to pay until 1946 some three per cent of the five per cent interest on up to £9.9 million of the costs, which made a tremendous difference to the viability of the scheme as a whole. The Underground Group was mindful of how traffic had built up so rapidly on the recently opened Morden extension and was confident that the same would happen on the Piccadilly, and after 1946 the extensions and improvements would be 'paying their way'. Traffic estimates for the northern extension 'were indicating ridership of 34 million a year when traffic had fully developed'.

By January 1934 it was estimated that 25 million people were using the northern extension, taken over the previous year, Manor House and Wood Green being the busiest; overall, some 44 per cent of users were thought to be drawn from a mile or more from a station, many using trams or buses from farther afield. In the more remote areas at the northern end there was some temporary excitement upon opening, but development was quite slow to take off. In Southgate some 30 firms of developers were busying themselves in 1934, each with their own style and aiming for subtly different markets. The centuries-old rural way of life was snuffed out within a couple of years as new roads were laid out and bricks filled up the landscape. Land to the north was gradually developed as the larger estate owners sold out one by one, though it was not until 1938 that one of the larger remaining plots at Southgate was swallowed up. Almost the whole area of developable land had been exploited before war broke out, except the tracts north-east of the Enfield West–Cockfosters section, which were blighted by wartime and post-war planning restrictions and even today are rural, though not necessarily agricultural. Even so, by 1951 when development had stabilized, there were 70 million annual users of the Cockfosters extension; this was double the original forecasts and more than justified the financial outlay.

At the west end of the Piccadilly, growth was probably more dramatic as the areas served by the railway were to an extent already established communities, albeit mainly low density. Even so, traffic was a little slower to develop during the first year than was hoped, owing, it was thought, to the high levels of unemployment. Nevertheless, total users of the South Harrow line had risen from 12.25 million in 1931 to 16.5 million in 1933, with traffic at Alperton rising by 71 per cent. This branch was particularly successful at attracting interchange from other forms of transport, thought to be as high as 30 per cent, compared with only 14 per cent on the Hounslow branch where traffic was much slower to develop. The new LPTB was happy to report a significant transfer of traffic from the District to the Piccadilly trains, releasing capacity thought likely to stimulate new growth on the District Line too. House-builders were anxious to grab the remaining land within walking distance of the Piccadilly western extension stations and by 1938 this process was all but complete and frequent Piccadilly trains were running with quite full loads. New districts such as Rayners Lane simply sprang up from open fields within four years. It is noteworthy that the population of outlying districts through which the north end of the Piccadilly passed grew by 26 per cent between 1931 and 1938, while the equivalent districts at the west end (including Uxbridge branch stations) grew by 61 per cent.

The Piccadilly Line entered a further long period of stability once the 1930s extensions were complete. A short-lived improvement included the arrival in 1936 of 24 experimental motor cars, 18 of which had streamlined driving cabs (this was a development from the single 'experimental' train proposal mentioned earlier). The cars ran as 4-car or 6-car trains, and while all cars were motor cars, only one axle of each pair on a truck was motored. The main advantage of the new cars was that in placing all the control equipment and the motors entirely under the car floor, the wasteful equipment compartments behind the driving cabs could be eliminated – together, this space amounted to the carrying capacity of one entire car. In addition it allowed a second double doorway to be fitted to motor cars, much improving boarding times. Although these particular trains were not very reliable, the design formed the basis of the ultimately successful 1938 stock which, for many years, was to be the mainstay of Northern and Bakerloo Line train services. The experimental cars were withdrawn at the outbreak of the Second World War, though they emerged again later after drastic modification.

One of the experimental trains near North Ealing comprising four of the streamlined cars. Just before war broke out three experimental trains were scheduled, 6-car in the peaks and 4-car off-peak.

One of the three flat-fronted experimental units showing how the front had been restyled to produce a conventional cab; the extra space thereby generated resulted in two more seats in the passenger compartment.

Soon after war broke out it became clear that shelterers needed basic facilities, and bunks, toilets and medical posts had all to be provided at low level.

WARTIME AND POST-WAR RECOVERY

When what was to become the Second World War broke out on 3rd September 1939, the LPTB had been planning for this eventuality for over two years and in expectation of immediate bombing a wartime organization structure came into being immediately. Engineering departments, in particular, were reorganized to deal with the effects of bomb damage and gas attacks, with huge resources made available to effect emergency repairs and maintain train services; emergency communications equipment was installed duplicating or triplicating existing critical telephone lines and serving a host of hastily established wartime offices and control rooms set up all around the network – if any of these were knocked out, an equivalent control elsewhere on the network could take over. An LPTB air raid precautions organization was also trained during this period to help with rescue arrangements in the aftermath of raids on transport infrastructure. Bombing within the London area did not in fact begin until about a year later which gave the organization a valuable breathing space to implement a host of preliminary measures, such as removal of prominent signs, and imposition of an efficient blackout arrangement on trains and stations, and even colour light signals were fitted with deeper lens hoods to restrict visibility from aircrafts at night as they would give away the position of railway lines. Most tube stations on the Piccadilly, in common with other lines, were subjected to the various temporary wartime works included building blast walls outside station entrances (reducing effects from nearby bomb explosions and reducing escape of light from entrances at night), and covering up or blocking up windows to reduce effects of flying

During the Second World War, Wood Green, like other below-ground stations, was equipped with blast walls along or just outside the entrances to reduce the effects of blast from a nearby bomb, and to support the blackout by restricted light emission from ticket halls at night.

Wartime restrictions resulted in removal of many large signs or their replacement for the duration by smaller versions so that locations would be harder to identify from enemy aircraft. Lighting was also seriously reduced and this sign has acquired its own low-powered floodlight.

glass or to provide modest safe sheltering for staff. Reduced lighting was a real problem for a public transport system and at some stations ingenuity was required to provide light adequate to keep stations safe to use at all; where station entrances comprised street stairwells they were finally covered over early in 1943 so that proper lighting could be provided without it being visible from above.

Lighting on trains was at first switched off at night in the open air, but this unsatisfactory solution was eased by fitting all cars with three dim blue lamps which provided a degree of visibility – these were later supplemented by heavily shrouded reading lamps whose light was not cast through the gaps in the window netting (provided to avoid splintering glass, but also reducing light output at night).

With war apparently inevitable, the Underground played its part in the mass evacuation of children which began on 1st September and concluded months of immaculate planning. The plan involved the operation of hundreds of special main line trains to take the children to a range of country distribution hubs from which they could be billeted using local transport. Most of the trains started at suburban stations such as Ealing Broadway (the busiest) and New Barnet, and a heavy burden was placed on the Piccadilly Line in helping to shift loads to the western end of the line and to Oakwood, from which convoys of children were shifted by special buses to New Barnet. Altogether 200,000 children were evacuated in four days. The inevitability of war simultaneously resulted in the closure of a number of central London stations to install watertight doors that could be closed if bomb damage caused flooding. Arsenal, Green Park, Hyde Park Corner, King's Cross and Knightsbridge were each affected and the last station reopened on 5th December. Flood prevention works also took place elsewhere, as did rearranging the ventilation system to reduce the danger from gas attacks, but these did not require station closure.

The start of London bombing inevitably gave rise to a popular belief that the tubes, being underground, were safe places to shelter. This feeling was at odds with a prevailing government direction that the tubes must on no account be used for sheltering, but it was impossible in practice to differential shelterers (who usually bought a penny ticket) from genuine passengers, and the authorities soon backtracked from the official position and began to make organized provision for regular sheltering. This included equipping platform areas with thousands of beds, arranged rows of 3-high bunks fixed against the walls, as well as toilets, sewage removal equipment and first aid posts. The situation was initially chaotic, and in October white lines were painted along the platforms both 4ft and 5ft from the platform edge. Shelter space could not officially be booked until 4.30pm behind the line, and after 7.30pm behind the 4ft line, leaving a narrow strip available for the travelling public. Tickets were eventually available on a nightly basis, but local authorities (with whom the LPTB worked very closely) also issued season tickets. It says something for British stoicism that this arrangement worked as well as it did for over a year, and again when the V1 and V2 rockets began to fall. Although the tubes were relatively safe, some stations were hit and generated casualties. The Piccadilly was particularly unfortunate at Bounds Green, where on 13th October 1940 a bomb explosion penetrated a platform tunnel, causing immense damage and filling much of the void with spoil. Nineteen shelterers died with many more seriously injured, and the train service was interrupted for two months.

The war resulted in several Piccadilly Line locations being put to alternative uses. In 1938 it was realized that, in wartime, government control of the railways would be necessary, and in the Munich crisis of 1938 a Railway Executive Committee was formed in preparation – though not initially with executive powers. Early in 1939 it was decided to make their wartime headquarters at Down Street station, where the lower areas were relatively safe from bombing. The disused entrance was heavily protected against bomb blast and gas attack and the former lift shaft was capped over

The lower portions of Down Street station were converted into offices for the wartime Railway Executive Committee, seen here at a meeting in April 1940. This conference room was also used occasionally by the War Cabinet.

Piccadilly Circus was the first station on the Underground to have its platforms fitted with fluorescent lighting, seen in this photograph taken shortly after the war. The standard stock train shows evidence of the enforced neglect of its paintwork.

with concrete, a small lift being installed in the stair-shaft. At low level, one of the lower lift landing passages was converted into the Committee's working area, with offices and a conference room. At platform level soundproofed walls were built to screen off the trains, and offices, kitchens, messing areas and dormitories were built. Anticipating war, the Committee assumed control of the main line railways and the LPTB on 1st September 1939, and Down Street was occupied immediately, though it wasn't quite complete. The wartime Cabinet was later to be an occasional visitor.

At Brompton Road similar considerations for a safe bomb-proof area led to the lower lift landings and lift shaft base being converted into an anti-aircraft operations room, the shape lending itself quite well to its new function; this remained in active use during the 1950s. At Green Park the disused Dover Street accommodation was occupied by LPTB staff, in common with some other stations, including Hyde Park Corner. At Aldwych the shuttle train service was suspended from September 1940 (until July 1946) and part of the line was used as a public shelter, other parts providing secure accommodation for British Museum objects. At Holborn both the Aldwych branch platforms were put to wartime use at part of its wartime engineering headquarters. In the western tunnel suites of offices, a dormitory and kitchen were built, on a single level on the old platform and split level over the track bed; for some years after the war this tunnel became a hostel for otherwise homeless staff. Also at Holborn an escalator from the upper flight was 'loaned' to HM Government for use in a wartime underground Wiltshire factory; it was subsequently replaced. At Earl's Court part of the 'intermediate' areas (the level between District and Piccadilly Lines) was used as a factory to make, amongst other things, torpedo sights.

With the war over, much-increased traffic levels required service improvements and additional rolling stock throughout the system. A few trains were made available by pressing into service cars which had been stored in the war owing to some of the new works extensions being postponed. Although the bulk of the stored cars were required for the Central Line extensions, it was clear that there would for a while be a modest quantity of surplus stock. From 1951 some 91 additional cars of the 1938 stock type were delivered to allow a comprehensive re-allocation of trains and enhanced services. Known as the 1949 stock, it comprised uncoupling non-driving motor and trailer cars and was not a self-contained fleet. Together with 18 rebuilt cars from the 1936 experimental batch and unused 1938 stock cars rendered surplus by changes of plan resulting from the war, it proved possible to generate a number of additional 7-car trains. One result was the Piccadilly receiving 15 trains of 1938 stock to augment its fleet of older generation trains, a few of which went to other lines using the same type of cars. The operating characteristics of the new trains had to be altered to match the old stock, and so far as possible they were run in convoys at the height of the peaks when their higher carrying capacity proved useful. The 1938 stock on the Piccadilly Line was formed into semi-permanently coupled 3-car or 4-car units. The 4-car unit contained two motor cars with a driving position, one motor car without a driving position (known as a non-driving motor car), and a trailer. The 3-car unit comprised one motor car with driving position, one trailer, and a motor car with uncoupling facilities and a 'shunting' driving position normally concealed behind a panel in the car bulkhead. The 4-car units could (and did) operate as short trains off-peak, while the 3-car units could not on their own be used in passenger service.

On the left is a Piccadilly Line 1938 stock driving motor car; this was the first production stock where the control equipment was beneath floor level; the larger number of motors rendered it unnecessary for them to come above floor level so for the first time the whole of the car was given over to passenger accommodation—except for the driving cab itself. The trains were for the first time arranged in semi-permanent units of 3-car or 4-car units, with fully automatic couplers at each end of the unit. On the right is a 1949 'uncoupling' non-driving motor car. It lacks driving cab but simplified controls were built into the end panelling allowing the unit to be moved around in depots. This arrangement confined these cars to the middle positions in full-length trains, with the units stabling off-peak. This picture was taken on 18th November 1952 and these trains operated on the Piccadilly Line from 1952 to 1975.

Typical pre-1938 stock of varying ages of car leaving South Harrow on 27th May 1956. Clearly seen is the relationship between the old station (centre) and the new building on far left. The 1903 signal cabin (still operating some pointwork mechanically) was replaced by remote controlled power-worked equipment the following year, and was demolished soon after.

To allow services to be improved, the signalling was enhanced at many stations with the introduction of 'speed control'. This relied on speed limit signs, speed sensing devices and additional signals, and the intention was to allow a train to proceed (safely) towards an occupied platform without being brought to a stand before the previous train departed – reducing headways in the process. By the end of 1946 the last remaining moving-spectacle tunnel signals on the Piccadilly had been replaced, and in November 1953 (near Ealing Common) the last electro-pneumatic semaphore signal was replaced by a coloured light signal. Minor station improvements were also made, not least of which was the removal of wartime equipment. At Leicester Square a new low level passage was built to improve interchange with the Northern Line, this opening on 5th July 1948.

When reopened in 1946, the Aldwych branch was notionally still worked by the double-ended 1906 cars with operation much on pre-war lines. In reality it seems these antiquarian cars had a short remaining life on this line and their appearance became increasingly sporadic, with 2-car trains of 'standard' stock soon scheduled (cars built between 1923 and 1934 were broadly interchangeable and had become known as standard stock). The French cars were not scrapped but from the late 1940s were used as so-called pilot cars for stock transfers and sometimes operated stores trains on the Piccadilly and Bakerloo Lines. They were finally withdrawn in December 1956. In 1954 two 2-car trains of the 1936 prototype batch of rolling stock (modernized) were made available to operate the Aldwych service. The unstreamlined cars had been set aside after the war for use as shuttle trains between Loughton and Epping, but this use had not proved necessary and they were more beneficially used on the Aldwych branch where they avoided tying up normal stock. In 1955 one of these cars was badly damaged in a collision at Aldwych, though it was subsequently repaired. From 1957 these cars were needed to service the Epping-Ongar branch and a 2-car standard stock train was again substituted.

On the main line the advantages of the improved equipment and enhanced capacity of the 1938 stock meant that by the early 1950s there were plans for a rolling programme to replace trains of older design. By this time the engineers were also keen to build car bodies from aluminium alloy, which was lighter than steel and at that time was more readily available. The Central Line, which had the oldest stock, was to have been the first to receive the new trains, followed by the Piccadilly. This new generation of trains was to have been known as the 1952 stock. The more advanced design drawings show that trains were at least at first planned to consist of new motor cars running with existing (but fully modernized) trailers. Although the scheme reached a very advanced stage of design, the time was not quite right and the replacement programme was postponed. Both the initial cost and some doubts about the ability of the substation capacity to meet demand contributed to its demise.

Things looked more hopeful in 1956 when three experimental trains were ordered from different manufacturers as a pilot for a new generation of stock. The manufacturers were Metropolitan-Cammell, Birmingham, and Gloucester, and the trains, though notionally similar, differed in detail from each other. Although built in aluminium alloy, they bore little obvious similarity with the proposed 1952 stock and a striking resemblance to the 1938/49 stock, with some updating. Principal differences included a new internal colour scheme, fluorescent lighting, rubber suspension (rather than springs), some minor equipment modifications and a destination blind display, which required the loss of the semi-streamlined roof dome. Fully automatic couplers were provided only at the middle of the train, with simplified couplers at the outer end for use only in emergencies. The train formations were similar to the 1938 stock, although the 3-car units had driving motor cars at each end. The three trains entered service on the Piccadilly Line in 1957 and 1958.

Artist's impression (as at October 1954) of the new unpainted alloy stock destined for the Piccadilly Line.

The first of the three prototype trains to arrive was the Metro-Cammell set. This shows the train at Northfields being displayed for the press; the 'driver' is being thanked by London Transport's Chairman, Sir John Elliot, who had once been assistant editor of the *Evening Standard* and probably enjoyed these functions.

After testing had been completed, an order was placed with Metropolitan-Cammell for 76 seven-car trains to replace the entire Piccadilly Line pre-1938 stock fleet; the first train entered service on 14th December 1959, and was known as the 1959 stock. The trains were similar to the prototypes but had numerous differences in detail, most obviously, perhaps, the simplified headlight display (since the extensions had opened, trains had carried headlight codes so that even at a distance staff could tell where the train was due to go, but this feature was no longer necessary). Unlike the prototypes, fully automatic couplers were available at all driving cab positions (as on 1938 stock).

In the event, things did not quite turn out as planned. The Central Line was also to have had new trains, but these were to have been quite unlike those of the Piccadilly and more the logical development of the 1952 stock. They were to be 8-car trains consisting of driving motor cars of a completely new 'all axles motored' design running with thoroughly modernized 'standard' stock trailers. Three prototype trains had been built along these lines and were already operating on the Central. Unfortunately, serious practical problems were encountered with this proposal, with the result that delivery of the new design was subjected to unacceptable delays.

The immediate challenge was that the Central's existing trains were now highly unreliable. What made things worse were rising traffic forecasts as imminent electrification of connecting British Rail lines threatened to generate considerable new business. This moved the priority for new stock from the Piccadilly to the Central Line, an immediate solution being found in switching delivery of the 1959 stock to the Central. In fact, the proposal for a new Central Line design was soon dropped altogether as the cost of converting the old trailers was higher than expected and there was some nervousness surrounding the unproven motor car design. As a result, a second batch of trains of similar type to the Piccadilly's 1959 stock was ordered (the 1962 stock), though incorporating some minor improvements.

Once the nineteenth new 1959 stock train had been put into service on the Piccadilly Line, the remaining deliveries were made to the Central, coming into service from July 1960. There were complications. The Central Line required 8-car trains while the 1959 stock trains were only 7-cars long. This shortcoming was covered by the car builders producing an additional 57 non-driving motor cars (nominally an advanced guard of 1962 stock) which were used to lengthen the 1959 stock trains. The Central Line's 1962 stock arrived between April 1962 and May 1964, allowing the 1959 stock to be moved to its true home on the Piccadilly Line (less the 57 additional non-driving motor cars), a process completed by June 1964. The three 1956 prototype trains were then modified to be fully compatible with the production batch. A single 3-car unit of 1962 stock was ordered and delivered for use on the Aldwych shuttle service to replace the 2-car train of standard stock; it would have been inconvenient to retain these odd cars but a train was not at first ordered without certainty the line would remain open. The Piccadilly retained its fifteen 1938 stock trains.

Between January and June 1951 an experiment was undertaken to place the guard in the centre of the 7-car train, rather than on the rear car, in order to have better supervision of passengers. This idea was not finally thought worth pursuing as it introduced as many problems as it solved.

The Piccadilly had abandoned the operation of short off-peak trains (a process called 'uncoupling') at the beginning of the Second World War but decided there were maintenance savings to be achieved and reintroduced the practice in May 1952. As previously, the practice was to run 4-car trains at quiet times and 7-car trains during peak hours. From 12th May the 3-car (east end) portion was uncoupled in off-peak periods and on Sundays and taken to sidings or one of the two depots. The uncoupling was normally done at Northfields in either of the westbound platforms (with coupling up in either eastbound platform), at Uxbridge, Arnos Grove, for trains reversing there, and Cockfosters. This broadly followed the pre-war pattern with the addition of Uxbridge as an uncoupling point. There was a small difference in these arrangements on Sundays when uncoupling and coupling was undertaken at South Harrow (either platform) but not at Arnos Grove. From mid-1958 two 1956 stock trains uncoupled with both the 4-car and the 3-car portions remaining in service.

The arrangements inevitably complicated the scheduling and train operating processes, especially with the incompatible 1938 stock trains joining in. The advent of newer trains with automatic couplers might have eased matters a little, but the decision was taken to abandon uncoupling from March 1960 (all tube lines had abandoned uncoupling by 1964). Short but frequent trains had their attractions but in practice required stopping marks carefully placed so that short trains would stop near to station entrances and exits. Those not in the know had occasionally to run half the length of a platform if they did not realize what was happening.

Hounslow West old station in the final phase of its existence with the approaches reduced to single track. The new route is on the right and at a lower level, and at this point there is a clear run into the new eastbound tunnel but the route to the westbound tunnel is obstructed by the old formation. All the old track and much of the formation from a point before the end of the old island platform, as far as the junction with the new route, had to be removed on the changeover weekend. The new cable run is already in place.

VICTORIA LINE AND HEATHROW

The building of the Victoria Line in the mid-1960s was to have a significant impact on the Piccadilly. The new line met the old at Finsbury Park, King's Cross and Green Park and was conceived in part to offer relief to a line that had long since been regarded as rather overcrowded. For a while there was even a debate about whether relief should include the Victoria Line serving Manor House instead of the Piccadilly, but extra cost and limited benefits made it not worthwhile. Good interchange at Finsbury Park was vital. By removing the old Northern City Line service and switching it to surface level platforms, two parallel low level platforms at Finsbury Park could be released. By diverting the westbound Piccadilly through one of these, the Victoria Line would be able to achieve same-level interchange in like directions by using the two other platforms. The Northern City Line was curtailed at Drayton Park in October 1964 and it took another 13 years before it was hooked up to the newly electrified Great Northern suburban electric services to serve Finsbury Park again.

Work began on the 3,150ft Piccadilly diversion tunnels early in 1964. The diversion was to connect with the existing line at so-called step-plate junctions. These had to be constructed around the existing tunnels using progressively larger tunnel segment diameters until at one end there was room for two running tunnels to join; when the junction tunnel was to complete the old running tunnel was dismantled from the top and the weight of the track progressively shifted from the old tunnel iron (which was removed) to new concrete trackbed. This work was necessarily very intricate as it involved diversion or protection of much cabling as well as the track. Once constructed, and with track and signalling already installed, the northern end connection with the existing line was switched simply by altering the temporary pointwork and changing over the signalling connections. At the southern end things were more interesting. The Piccadilly diversion had to dip sharply beneath the new Victoria Line northbound tunnel and met the existing Piccadilly with a 5 foot difference in level where the old and new routes entered the southern junction tunnel, about 200ft north of Arsenal station. This required the old line to be supported on a massive trestle which dropped down from the entry end of the step plate to the new level at the exit (narrow) end. On the day of the changeover the trestle had to be demolished and its remains and old track entirely removed; the new track had then to be laid in on the new alignment to connect with that already laid in the diversion tunnel – an intensive task completed by 2pm on Sunday 3rd October 1965, having started at close of traffic on Saturday night. The old tunnel was then entirely stripped out and the old platform was made ready to receive the new line.

Hounslow East station had changed very little since its opening (as Hounslow Town) in 1909, though the waiting room (and there would have been a lot of waiting until the Piccadilly got through) has been expanded at some point. This station lacked almost every facility until rebuilt in 1963. In the distance in the first photo (taken in the late 1930s) is the substation; the old Hounslow Town branch ran round the far side of this. Although hard to imagine, the ferociously sharp and short-lived connecting curve between Heston and Hounslow Town peeled off to the right more or less at the point from which these photos were taken. The second photo is of Hounslow East on 8th October 1965 showing the newly rebuilt facilities.

At King's Cross the Northern and Piccadilly Line ticket hall was less than thirty years old but had now to be adapted to handle Victoria Line traffic. Expansion was very difficult but some enlargement was possible and two new escalators and a fixed stairway were squeezed in that gave direct access to the Victoria Line lower concourse. Interchange stairs were also put in between that level and the deeper Piccadilly Line level almost underneath. At Green Park same-level interchange with the Piccadilly was impossible as the lines crossed at right angles; to reduce risks of platform level overcrowding, the stairs to the long-disused Dover Street exit were renovated and connected into a long and dreary subway that effectively took passengers back along the platform to the point where it was convenient to link into the Victoria Line. However, the ticket hall was considerably enlarged to accommodate new Victoria Line escalators which were close to those for the Piccadilly, and many passengers chose that as the natural interchange route. A Victoria Line substation was built in the old Dover Street station lift shafts. The Victoria Line opened on 1st September 1968 from Walthamstow to Highbury, extended to Warren Street on 1st December and Victoria on 7th March 1969. It considerably altered traffic patterns on the network and, as planned, provided welcome relief to the Piccadilly. The new line is connected with the Piccadilly at junctions south of Finsbury Park but the links are only used for engineering trains and stock movement.

London Underground's link to Heathrow Airport took many years to achieve, and many ideas were examined. Given the airport's strategic importance to London in general and the Underground in particular, it may be helpful to see how the airport developed, together with its transport access.

Prior to the Second World War London's main airport was at Croydon, which was opened in March 1920 and expanded rapidly. Over the following decade a few other aerodromes around London's periphery were used as regional airports, including Heston and (from 1935) Gatwick. Some international traffic was handled by the flying boat service from Southampton. Passenger accommodation on the aircraft of the day was small, and only exceeded single figures from the mid-1930s. The relative closeness of the airports to London, and the small loadings, made transport between the airport and the centre of London fairly easy, and suitably adapted coaches (sometimes on motor car chassis) were used. The prevailing view was that air transport was essentially a city-centre to city-centre business, and that passengers were transmitted between in-town offices, with some of the intervening journey being by road and some in the air. In any case, volumes were still tiny and well within the capacity of uncongested new arterial roads.

With the airline business expanding rapidly, a pressing need emerged for substantially larger airports capable of handling the growing number of flights and the larger, heavier aircraft which were being developed. The proposals put in hand intended there to be four London Airports. Two of these already existed, with Heston to be much enlarged and Croydon to be fully modernized. A third was intended at a new site at Lullingstone, in Kent, while the fourth was to be operated by the City of London and located at Fairlop, in Essex. Both Lullingstone and Fairlop were to be rail connected (the station at Lullingstone was built but never opened, and plans were developed for Fairlop): there was no doubt in anyone's mind about the benefits of rapid access to central London.

The war precipitated a major change of direction. It became obvious that aircraft development was proceeding very rapidly indeed and that aeroplanes were going to be somewhat bigger than the pre-war plans had anticipated and would require very long concrete runways. The outcome of this was the decision to use a single site at Heathrow, using as its core a massive but part-complete military transport aerodrome on requisitioned land. This site was handed over to the civil authorities on 1st January 1946. Even then, only the main runway was operational and there was considerable work to do on the others. The control tower, but no terminal buildings, was ready, and this allowed very limited use to be made by civil aircraft. It was not until the end of May that the airport was fully opened for traffic. Even then, only long-haul flights were made from Heathrow, and European services found a home at Northolt airport until they transferred to Heathrow in 1955.

The plan was to concentrate all passenger facilities in the centre of the airport (although temporary terminal buildings were eventually built on the northern edge by the Bath Road). Progress was very slow and the central area facilities only became operational in 1955, and then did not handle all passenger requirements until 1961 when the north terminal was replaced by a new 'Terminal 1' in the central area. The third terminal building in the central area opened in 1968 (allowing the older buildings to be renovated). The rate of growth of traffic to the airport was phenomenal. In 1953 the annual traffic handled at Heathrow exceeded one million for the first time. By 1973 the annual traffic exceeded twenty million passengers, an average rise of a million passengers each year. To this heavy traffic must be added the vast stream of visitors and friends who visited the airport (nearly another million), and an ever-growing number of airport staff (then over 50,000). Virtually all this traffic came by road.

Even in the mid-1970s the transport philosophy had not in principle changed from its pre-war view that air travel was a between city-centre activity, and airline passengers were still booked in at air terminals near central London and transported to the airport in buses run by the airlines (in 1948 only 25 per cent of passengers made their own way to the airport). But airline coaches became an increasing problem. First, the Police and Traffic Commissioners were antagonistic towards airline terminals in the heart of the West End or City, and while the BOAC terminal at Victoria was not entirely inconvenient, the new BEA terminal at Cromwell Road (opened 1957) was not particularly well located. If public transport (and then a difficult walk if one had luggage) had to be used to get to the terminals, it was not much more difficult to get straight to Heathrow by changing onto a bus at, for example, Hounslow. Secondly, the nature of airline travel was changing with increasing business and leisure traffic creating an enlarging body of customers not anxious to pass through central London. Thirdly, the need to meet increasingly large aircraft meant that it was becoming logistically more difficult to manage the coach link operation, and in any case traffic congestion was making the airline coach links very much less reliable.

For these reasons it is possible during the 1960s and 1970s not only to identify a huge increase in self-drive or taxi airport traffic, but also to note a distinct shift towards booking in at the airport rather than a town terminal, requiring airport facilities to be improved accordingly (which partly duplicated the work of the in-town terminals and increased costs).

Until 1969 only the airline coaches provided dedicated air-passenger access to Heathrow, though a number of London Transport bus routes had always served the airport in one way or another. In response to demand, in August 1969 bus services in the Hounslow area were reorganized and a new route (the A1 Express) was established between the Airport central bus station (reasonably near all three terminals) and Hounslow West Piccadilly Line station. This operated at a flat fare and vehicles had some luggage space. Through fares were not available from the Underground, although joint marketing of the service became a feature, and the bus stop was right outside the station where covered waiting was available.

At first sight it is surprising that rail access seemed to command such little priority post-war when it was deemed such a key feature pre-war. Even Gatwick, which was rail served, was slow to re-emerge after the war (though it might not have done at all had it not had good rail access). In fact, rail access to Heathrow had been contemplated from its earliest civilian days. Schemes included a Southern Railway spur from Feltham, a dedicated deep level tube line, and a Piccadilly Line extension from Hounslow West. The appalling shortage of capital, labour and materials, coupled with initially slow development at the airport itself, and the apparently adequate road services (using the new Cromwell Road, and later the M4 motorway), all served to lower the priority of direct rail access. Why was it not until the 1960s that the long-term inevitability of a high capacity transport access system was seriously addressed? It is worth examining the emergence of the final scheme.

During the summer of 1946 there had been some discussion in the press suggesting a railway line from the airport to the London–Staines line of the Southern. A year later Twickenham Corporation was informed by the Ministry of Town and Country Planning that it was proposing to construct a rail link to London Airport; the new line was to join the Southern about 300 yards west of Feltham station.

London Transport's view was inconsistent. Towards the end of 1946 it had reviewed possible direct rail access between the airport and a new terminal at one of two sites: Cromwell Road (near Earl's Court) or another site north of Hyde Park. The provision of such an express railway would cost between £5 million and £12 million, it was said, but would offer journey times of 15–20 minutes. Its 'official' stance was that on such a railway it would be 'impossible' to accommodate both airline users and ordinary passengers. For ordinary use there would be conflicting requirements for additional intermediate stations and the problems of rush hour crowding to contend with, and this would destroy its benefit to airline users. On the other hand, an express tube would be difficult to justify financially if it were to rely on airline users alone. Cheaper alternatives such as a form of overhead railway were dismissed as 'a retrograde step from the standpoint of good town planning' (a matter which was later ignored when the M4 motorway access from central London to Heathrow was being developed). London Transport's link to Heathrow was therefore accepted as being confined to the supply of contract coaches – an operation lasting for nearly thirty years more.

Hounslow West terminus in the 1950s while extension to Heathrow was being debated. The island platform in the foreground was added in 1926 when the track from Hounslow Central was doubled, but the position of the original platform is also visible. Although the platforms were below street level, the angle was awkward for direct projection of the line and new platforms were built a little to the north. Virtually the whole of this area is now under the station car park.

Perhaps in contrast, by March 1947 London Transport had developed its own tentative plan in an attempt to take a more realistic planning view. Of several new routes suggested, Route K (a variation of the London Plan Route 5) proposed a new tube line making a junction with the Central Line at Marble Arch. It would then run as a high speed tube to North Acton, making another interchange with the Central Line to Ruislip, and then take over the Ealing branch, extending to Southall and Windsor over the GWR. A branch would be built from Southall to London Airport, and the proposed service level was 16 trains per hour.

At around the same time, the Standing Joint Committee of the main line railways and the LPTB were, at the Government's request, also contemplating London's transport requirements, again choosing to ignore the unrealistic suggestions of the London Plan Committee. The Joint Committee put forward some 22 railway schemes, including two main line tube railways designed both to ease London traffic and serve the site of the proposed World Fair at Osterley Park in 1951, at a combined cost of £45 million. Enormous cost, and quite unrealistic demands on scarce construction materials, characterized many schemes of this period.

Of these proposals, tube route 'A' was to run to Osterley from Liverpool Street, largely shadowing the Central Line, while tube route 'B' would run from King's Cross via Victoria and Cromwell Road (which was one of the proposed sites for a new air terminal, though it would make re-arrangement of tracks between South Kensington and Earl's Court a priority, at a further cost of £2 million). It was noted that both new lines would improve access to Heathrow Airport, and that route 'B' could be extended to the airport itself for a further £6 million or so. The World Fair did not, of course, take place at Osterley and was absorbed into what became the Festival of Britain, focusing on Waterloo. There were no new tube lines, but of the little transport infrastructure actually provided for the festival were included a pair of escalators at Waterloo, later to be used, with perhaps some irony, to serve the Waterloo BEA air terminal from where passengers were taken by bus to the airport.

An internal London Transport report of 1948 noted the importance both of the proposed express tube schemes, and of the need to serve the airport, but preferred a more realistic option. An extension of the Hounslow branch to London Airport was seen as the solution. However, the point was made that the airport was 'too far out to suffer at the hands of an "all stations" service', and it suggested that airport trains should run substantially 'non stop', which could be achieved by extending the four-tracking from Northfields to Hounslow East. The observation was made that the District Line trains had a higher capacity and rode somewhat better than those of the Piccadilly Line, and proposed that it be the District Line which was extended to the airport.

The nationalization of transport in 1948 saw the end of the Standing Joint Committee (and its main line tube proposals) but introduced the British Transport Commission (BTC), to whom London Transport reported and who might reasonably be expected to have a view. Another committee was thus set up, reporting the BTC's view in 1949. This proposed a range of transport options for London but failed to attribute a link to the airport as requiring high priority, though noting that its proposed 'route D' required an outlet in west London, 'the exact route to be determined in relationship with western branches of District Line and London Airport'. The low priority and heavy investment demands were to see this scheme die completely in 1955.

The absence of a sound proposal from the nationalized transport system evidently caused others to contemplate schemes. For example, there was a 1958 proposal for a privately sponsored rapid transport system to link London and Heathrow called Air-Rail. This was a scheme for a high-speed monorail broadly spanning the Southern Region route to Feltham. The monorail cars (described as being similar to Green Line coaches) were to have the ability to leave the monorail system at the airport and manoeuvre around the terminals by road. Perhaps unsurprisingly this came to nought, but it is indicative of the frustration at the lack of 'official' initiative.

By the early 1960s both LT and BR were considering firm schemes; any element of competition between their proposals was heightened by the abolition of the BTC in 1963 and the establishment of BR and LT as separate nationalized boards. LT pressed for their (now Piccadilly Line) extension from Hounslow; earlier concerns about the incompatible nature of the traffics, or the preference for the larger District-style rolling stock, being publicly overlooked (indeed the District service to Hounslow was abandoned in 1964). The scheme emerging from the Southern Region of BR had originally envisaged dedicated tracks to Victoria but this had been revised (to keep costs down) such that only the airport spur would be dedicated and the trains would interwork with the normal service east of Feltham – though they would be exclusive to air passengers and airport visitors. Even so, the notional cost would be £14 million, and this sum would be hard to find in the middle of the BR modernization programme.

By June 1964 the Ministry of Civil Aviation, which ran the civil airports, was expressing interest in establishing Victoria as a central in-town terminal for Gatwick and Stansted (as well as Heathrow) and was increasingly interested in a direct rail link to Heathrow. This tended to favour the Southern Region alternative, though by then two firms of industrialists were submitting separate monorail schemes. By the end of the year London Transport had reaffirmed that if they extended to Heathrow from Hounslow, the branch would become part of the normal Underground system. Sadly, government funding regimes require things to be built down to a cost rather than up to a quality, but the alternative was thought to be nothing at all.

By February 1966 not only were the new Greater London Council and British Airports Authority both taking a keen interest in an airport rail link, but the airlines themselves (saddled with the supply of existing transport) were actively lobbying. BEA, in particular, was interested in the LT scheme – despite a threatened journey time of 43 minutes from Piccadilly to Heathrow. LT, for its part, felt an extension would only be viable if the existing coach services were abandoned. The Southern Region continued to nurse its own scheme. Later that year the BAA also adopted the LT scheme, but optimistically added that they felt the Southern Region scheme would be required as well (it didn't have to pay for it). It was, of course, recognized that funding for both schemes was unlikely, but the Government allowed a Bill for both proposals to be introduced that November for consideration in the next parliamentary session. Both received the Royal Assent on 27th July 1967.

The issue was now passed to the 'Transport Co-ordinating Council for London' who discussed the matter on 31st July 1967; both LT and BR were heavily represented. This time a comparative report came out in favour of the Southern Region scheme, but the advantages of the LT proposal were noted (and the BAA still wanted both extensions). The matter, once again, awaited government decision. Matters were not helped by a sudden resurgence of interest by the airlines in the proposed central terminal at Victoria (which would further have favoured the Southern Region link).

The BAA also expressed concern at the disruption the LT link might cause during construction (and the cost to BAA of the necessary ancillary works). These factors might have clinched a decision had it not been for LT in January 1968 unexpectedly telling the ministry that it had dropped its construction estimate by £1 million to £12.3 million 'as a result of more detailed examination'. LT was becoming positively enthusiastic.

Other factors were now becoming significant, not least of which was the imminent transfer of London Transport from government control to that of the Greater London Council, effective from January 1970. Government consent for an extension had still not been given by the time that the transfer had been effected, by which time yet more studies had been undertaken into the respective viability of the two schemes. This time the LT proposal was favoured, though with continuance of the dedicated airport coach links from the existing terminals. The GLC were quickly convinced, and authorized the Piccadilly Line extension on 7th July 1970, together with a quarter of the relevant funding. The matter still required the government go-ahead, which emerged on 6th November 1970, though without any financial contribution on the grounds that the works were expected to be profitable; LT had to fund the difference itself, although considerable pressure later resulted in a 25 per cent government contribution, authorized in April 1972.

Physical work on the Heathrow extension officially began on 27th April 1971 with a ceremony at which 'the first sod' was cut (with a bulldozer) by the leader of the Greater London Council, Sir Desmond Plummer (there is a rumour that a piqued Airport authority required the sod to be put back again afterwards to await a more convenient start of works).

There were to be only two stations on the 3.5 mile extension. The terminus was in the vicinity of the airline terminals in the centre of the airport complex, almost underneath the bus station. The intermediate station was to be at Hatton Cross, at the eastern perimeter which was intended primarily to serve airport maintenance workers – though a bus station would provide handy bus-rail interchange. However, the existing 3-platform open-air station at Hounslow West was badly located for the line's projection and it was decided to construct a new pair of platforms (this time sub-surface) slightly to the north, but linked to the 1931 ticket hall. The name of the airport station caused some controversy, but in the event 'Heathrow Central' was settled upon in preference to 'Heathrow Airport', though an aircraft symbol was usually incorporated as part of the name.

At Hounslow West the old brick signal box was on the line of route of the diverted tracks and required early demolition. Its place was taken from 26th March 1972 by a temporary wooden signal box next to the southern platform.

The 2-mile section between Hounslow West and Hatton Cross was built 'cut and cover', largely alongside or beneath the verges of the Bath Road and the Great South West Road. In contrast to the cut-and-cover type of construction a century previously, disruption was kept to a minimum using new methods. After excavating only a shallow trench, it was then possible to construct the tunnel walls and roof, subsequently removing the spoil from within the new shell through periodic access points. The walls consisted of a continuous run of intersecting concrete piles, and this proved to be a fast and effective method of construction. Just east of Hatton Cross the line had to negotiate the River Crane which it crossed by bridge, rising briefly to the surface either side in concrete retaining walls.

The section between Hatton Cross and Heathrow Central was constructed by traditional deep tube methods in twin tunnels. The station itself was built within a huge concrete box, excavated from the surface. This had walls over 3ft thick, and was around 400ft long, 80ft wide and 50ft deep. The box was designed to support future BAA construction at ground level. Within the box the platforms occupied the lowest level, station plant and staff rooms the next, and the upper level housed separate entry and exit flows through the ticket hall. Beyond the station the over-run tunnels pointed towards the West Middlesex sludge disposal works at Perry Oaks, then considered the most likely site for a fourth airline terminal, to which serious attention was beginning to turn.

At Hounslow West both the old District Railway signal box and the eastern end of Platform 3 (the northernmost platform track) obstructed the line of the extension, and in particular the temporary access track which was required. The platform was taken out of service on 22nd October 1971 whilst a temporary signal box was commissioned on the embankment adjacent to platform 1 on 26th March 1972, allowing demolition of the offending structure. The turnout to platform 3 was retained and linked to the temporary track connection used to provide access for tracklaying and materials trains. This link was removed about six weeks before the extension was commissioned to allow further excavation and other preparatory work to be undertaken, including track simplification.

The work required at the Heathrow end of the extension took much longer than that at the Hounslow end, and a phased opening was opportune, extension to Hatton Cross constituting a first phase. The Hatton Cross link began to carry passengers from start of traffic on Saturday 19th July 1975 when Hatton Cross opened to the public, without ceremony. Although the A1 express service continued to run between Hounslow West and the airport, a number of other bus services were adjusted to run through a new bus station at Hatton Cross, alongside the single storey station building which led down to the island platform beneath. The section between Hatton Cross and Heathrow Central was opened by the Queen on Friday 16th December 1977 shortly before midday, the section becoming available to the public from 3pm. The A1 express service was now withdrawn. Heathrow Central station was provided with an island platform layout, with escalators linking to the ticket hall area alongside (but below) the bus station and linked to the three terminal buildings with BAA-built moving walkways.

Each station had a new interlocking machine room supervised from Earl's Court control room. The power supply for trains on the Heathrow extension came from two new remote controlled substations at Hatton Cross and Heathrow Central, both fed from Lots Road power station.

For some years Heathrow Airport was one of a small number of destinations to which it was possible to book day return tickets which included the connecting bus journey. These facilities were withdrawn during the 1970s.

A significant addition to the line's route mileage was also going to mean more trains, and it will be useful to recall the prevailing rolling stock position at around 1970. The line had a holding of 79½ trains of 1956/59/62 stock and (in theory) 15 trains of 1938 stock, though the actual holding of the latter was to shrink rapidly as reliability deteriorated. Although the line was not next in the queue for new trains (it was the Northern) there were now thought to be advantages in switching priority to the Piccadilly to coincide with opening the prestigious airport extension. Quite apart from presenting a modern appearance to passengers emerging from modern airliners, the new trains could be better able to cope with accompanying luggage and it was hoped would also offer faster and more comfortable journeys. For technical reasons it was also looking more likely that one-person operation could be introduced more quickly if new stock entered service on the Piccadilly in preference to the Northern Line.

The main order for the new rolling stock was placed with Metropolitan-Cammell in November 1971. The trains were to be of six cars, but with each car around 6ft longer than conventional ones, the overall carrying capacity of a train was similar, though some reduction in seating was inevitable. The need for this arose from the planned one-person operation where it was necessary for the whole train (and particularly the drivers' cab) to be within platform limits when stopped at a platform – the existing 7-car trains were about 15ft too long: 6-car trains also had the advantage of avoiding asymmetrical trains composed of 4-car and 3-car units, which had an adverse effect on spares requirements. Like their predecessors, the trains were built of unpainted aluminium alloy, though internally unpainted plastic finishes were used where possible.

1973 tube stock train at Sudbury Hill.

Left The styling of the airport extension station platforms.

Below Hatton Cross was the furthest 1938 stock reached in service, but Heathrow labels for the destination plates were produced.

Bottom The opening of the Heathrow extension had the Queen taking a cab ride.

To reduce costs the majority of trains were built with no driving cabs in the middle, although they had semi-automatic couplers and shunting controls between the third and fourth cars to facilitate efficient maintenance on a 3-car unit basis. The outer cabs had only simplified mechanical couplers as they would only need to couple to anything in an emergency. A proportion of trains were built with semi-automatic couplers and driving cabs at each end of the 3-car units, and these units could therefore be used to substitute for either one of the single-ended units to facilitate maintenance and improve overall stock availability. These double-ended 3-car units could also operate as a 'train' on the Aldwych shuttle service, where further thoughts of closure had not come to anything. The numbers of trains ordered did actually fluctuate slightly, although 87½ was the number eventually settled upon. The cost of two trains was allocated to the Heathrow extension and the balance from the train renewal project. One train was used for some years to test experimental equipment.

Although a 1973 stock train was used on the day of the Hatton Cross opening, the first new train did not enter regular service until 18th August 1975 and this soon allowed the remaining three 1938 stock trains to be withdrawn or transferred (the last one operated on the Piccadilly on 2nd December 1975). Between November 1975 and October 1979 Piccadilly Line 1959 stock was transferred to the Northern Line, allowing 1938 stock to be withdrawn on that line. The last 1959 stock train ran on the Piccadilly Line on Friday 5th October 1979, although the 3-car unit of 1962 stock continued to operate on the Aldwych shuttle until 17th October.

The single platform (above) and the booking hall (below) at Heathrow Terminal 4.

HEATHROW TERMINALS 4 AND 5

Even while the Heathrow extension was being built, controversy was raging over the possibility of an additional London airport, or an additional fourth airline terminal at Heathrow. This culminated in a major planning inquiry during 1980. The outcome was a decision to build a vast new passenger terminal towards the south-east corner of the airport, just south of the southern runway.

If the new terminal were to be served by the Piccadilly Line, access was going to be a problem. Although it lay between Hatton Cross and Heathrow Central it was considerably to the south, ruling it out as an intermediate station. Options included constructing the Terminal 4 station on a branch from Hatton Cross, constructing a 'people-mover' at surface level between the new terminal and Hatton Cross, and abandoning the existing alignment completely between Hatton Cross and Heathrow Central and building a new route via Terminal 4. This would require virtually a new station at Heathrow Central. The planning inquiry inspector, appropriately named Glidewell, also considered a British Rail proposal for a line from Feltham.

In the event none of these options was adopted and a more revolutionary concept was proposed whereby a vast single track loop was constructed, branching off the existing Piccadilly Line just west of Hatton Cross to serve Terminal 4, and then continuing to the existing platforms at Heathrow Central, approaching them from the west through what had originally been the over-run tunnels. Trains would all run in a clockwise direction serving Terminal 4 and then Heathrow Central. The existing direct line between these two stations would become one-way in normal use, but with the westbound direct line available in emergency.

The proposal had the obvious objection that passengers wishing to travel from Heathrow Central to Terminal 4 would have to change at Hatton Cross, but the overall economy of the scheme greatly outweighed the inconvenience it would cause to a fairly small minority of users and was eventually accepted by all parties. The scheme would also add an extra five minutes journey time to passengers travelling towards Heathrow Central – a 10 per cent journey penalty on a journey from central London. Loss of normal reversing and layover time at Heathrow Central would be partly compensated by running trains alternately through each platform where some stand time could be built in, unfortunately increasing further the running time from Terminal 4 to Central London.

Parliamentary powers for the loop were obtained in the London Transport Act 1981, although a substantial deviation was authorized in the vicinity of Terminal 4 station the following year owing to the BAA rushing ahead with the main terminal building, thus forcing the Piccadilly station to a second-best location beneath the car park. The Secretary of State approved the loop scheme on 19th July 1982, and construction work was officially started at a ceremony on Wednesday 9th February 1983. The loop was to be roughly 3.5 miles long and was expected (in 1982) to cost £24.6 million, some £5.2 million of which was for Terminal 4 station itself. Despite original estimates, the strong desire for the new station to be opened at the same time as the terminal caused a major rethink in how the work should proceed, and a very short construction timescale was adopted. The tunnelling, for example, was to be undertaken in a 17-month programme. This left precious little time for track and signalling to be installed.

The ambitious timescale was achieved, and the loop was commissioned on Monday 4th November 1985. Unfortunately, delays in construction of the actual terminal by BAA contractors meant that to an extent this effort was wasted, negating the BAA's earlier haste. For several more months trains continued to use the existing route to Heathrow Central. The airline terminal and new station were eventually opened at a ceremony on Tuesday 1st April 1986, by the Prince and Princess of Wales. Public traffic began on Saturday 12th April 1986. On the same day Heathrow Central was renamed 'Heathrow Terminals 1,2,3', the new station being called 'Heathrow Terminal 4'. The latter had only a single platform and simple access to the main terminal building.

Since the 1960s, the supervision of signalling has gradually been centralized at a regulating room at Earl's Court. Most major junctions and scheduled reversing points are controlled automatically by equipment in which timetable information is stored, routes being set up physically by air-operated interlocking machines only accessible to technical staff.

On the section from Rayners Lane to Uxbridge (strictly speaking the Metropolitan Line) control of the signalling at both places is now centralized at Rayners Lane signal cabin where push-button equipment operates interlocking machines at each site. This cabin also controls a reversing point at Ruislip (installed in 1975) which is now used to reverse a proportion of the Piccadilly's Uxbridge line trains. All moves are set up by the signalman. Other than on this section, there are now no signal cabins on the Piccadilly Line. Latterly they were (with closure dates in brackets) at Cockfosters, Oakwood, Arnos Grove and Wood Green (all automated in 1982); Finsbury Park (reversing facilities decommissioned 1965), York Road (reversing facilities decommissioned 1964); King's Cross (remote control from Covent Garden – later from Earl's Court – 1962); Holborn (remote control from Earl's Court 1980); Covent Garden (reversing facilities decommissioned 1979); Hyde Park Corner (remote control from Earl's Court 1979); West Kensington West (1962); Hammersmith (programme machines 1963); Acton Town (programme machines 1965); Northfields (programme machines 1974); Hounslow Central (remote control from Earl's Court 1976); Hounslow West (terminal facilities decommissioned 1975); Ealing Common (programme machines 1960); South Harrow (push-button control from Rayners Lane 1957 and programme machines 1978). At Hatton Cross direct control is either exercised from Earl's Court or automatic reversing can be set up for trains to reverse west to east – a programme machine was provided during the brief period when this station was a terminal in order to keep trains to time and set up descriptions, but this was removed when the main service was extended to Heathrow. At King's Cross the connection to what had become the Northern Line was supplemented from 1956 by a trailing emergency crossover. At the time of closure in 1976 the cabin at Hounslow Central still had an original District Railway mechanical frame in situ, and the crossover was entirely mechanically operated; when the new equipment was installed the crossover was converted to electro-pneumatic operation controlled from Earl's Court. Most of the 1930s automatic signalling was also updated in the 1970s and early 1980s.

Power supply arrangements have been gradually updated since the 1930s reconstructions with all substations modernized; these now house solid-state equipment instead of mercury arc rectifiers or rotary converters, and they are now remotely controlled from a central point instead of regional control rooms. Some changes to supply sources have been made. The Cockfosters line is no longer supplied from the old NorthMet network and was transferred to the Lots Road supply. On the other hand the Ravenscourt Park to Uxbridge and Northfields sections were switched to supplies from the National Grid. The remaining sections of the line, including the Heathrow section, are all fed from what is still termed the London Underground supply. The logic for this was simply that the Lots Road supply was thought more reliable and was better suited for supplying the underground sections of line where loss of power could be very awkward. Under a private finance deal in 1998 a company called Seeboard (now EDF) Powerlink entered into a 30-year contract to operate, maintain, finance and renew the whole of the Underground's power supply equipment, and as part of this the ageing Lots Road was to be closed with all electricity bought in bulk from the grid; Lots Road breathed its last on 31st October 2003, and the site was redeveloped. Since then all traction power comes from a high tension network supplied from several National Grid bulk supply points in order to maintain high load security. To provide backup, all stations have lighting and other critical circuits supported by emergency batteries, and an emergency feed is maintained from the support power station at Greenwich which can be placed on line within 15 minutes.

Train maintenance is undertaken at the main depot at Northfields with light maintenance and cleaning also done at Cockfosters. For many years Underground stock also had to undergo major overhaul and repainting at 3–4 year intervals which gradually lengthened over the years. After unpainted alloy stock became standard, major overhaul was pushed out to around eight to nine years, and modern stock really only needs 'major' overhaul once during its life and in the case of the Piccadilly this was made to coincide with internal refurbishment and painting. The main driver for heavy overhaul was paint condition, reconditioning of seating, rewiring and removal and stripping down of moving parts. On modern trains moving and rubbing surfaces have been drastically reduced and modern wiring lasts far longer. Equipment can therefore be exchanged for float material in depots for repair on or off site as required. Heavy overhaul of Piccadilly trains was very awkward in the confines of Lillie Bridge and was at first undertaken in the District Railway's new depot at Ealing Common. In August 1921 a central overhaul works was opened at Acton Town, on the south side of the line, and after a few years heavy overhaul of the whole of the Underground's fleet was transferred here. Cars arrived and were cleaned, then entirely stripped down, rebuilt and repainted. During the 1980s, with overhauls becoming so extended, it was decided that the remaining work was well within the capability of maintenance depots, with equipment still requiring overhauling (like motors) being sent to Acton by road. On the Piccadilly Line, space and facilities for this activity were made available at Cockfosters and the first heavy overhaul there was completed in June 1986.

An interesting sideline of Piccadilly Line history results from its proximity to Acton overhaul works, where the rolling stock design function was located and where much experimental work was undertaken. The need to be able to test trains at speed made it necessary to undertake trials on running lines. Within only a couple of years of the 'western extensions' opening, it was obvious that four tracks between Acton and Northfields were quite unnecessary off-peak. Although the track layout at Acton Town condemned Piccadilly trains to use the centre tracks between those stations at busy times, in off-peak periods (when no District trains ran to Hounslow) all Piccadilly Hounslow branch trains could be switched to the outer tracks, leaving the centre pair available for train testing at speed with no risk of delaying passenger trains. These centre tracks were certainly used from early 1936 for such occasional activities – once test trains were locked into either line under 'possession' rules they could operate to and fro as required by the engineer in charge. After the war it became the practice to use the centre (or 'fast') tracks more and more for such purposes. The difficulties of testing brakes in wet conditions during dry weather caused equipment to be installed just after the war to allow the rails on the fast lines to be drenched with water by sprays fed by pipes along the track fed from a large tank. For a while in the early 1960s automatic train operation was tested on these test tracks. During the 1970s it was decided to convert one track into a permanent test facility and the eastbound local was selected, being withdrawn from passenger use from 4th November 1985. However, with train design and development being increasingly outsourced, the requirement for a dedicated track diminished and it was restored to normal service again in September 1995, though in fact it sees little use.

A Piccadilly Line oddity was the scheduled service to or from West Kensington on the District Line, run more for operational convenience than any other reason. Starting in 1933 one train early in the morning was scheduled to reverse east to west at West Kensington, returning as a staff train to Hammersmith where it went into passenger service. A few years later the train carried passengers all the way from West Kensington and had been joined by others, the later ones additionally carrying passengers towards West Kensington as well. Some late night staff trains had also appeared. In 1970 during the week, three early morning trains reversed at West Kensington, two of them returning in passenger service; there were also two late night staff-only trains. On Sunday mornings there was also a scheduled passenger train to West Kensington (and 1973 stock destination blinds provided for it). These workings survived until 27th October 1991, by which time there were two morning and one evening working. Another long-standing curiosity was the stabling of Piccadilly Line trains at Ealing Common and District Line trains at Northfields; for many years there were four of the former and five of the latter. Again, this was the result of operational convenience, mainly to allow District trains to come into service on the Hounslow branch. The position was regularized in 1964 when the withdrawal of District trains to Hounslow rendered the arrangement unnecessary.

All the original Piccadilly lifts have now been replaced by escalators or modern lift equipment. The Piccadilly's escalators have all been replaced or updated, although the original 1930s machines still survive (less the wooden panelling) at the Exhibition exit at Earl's Court, though they are rarely used. In 1955 an escalator was installed at Alperton to carry passengers up to the London-bound platform, the machine having been transferred from the Festival of Britain after its closure (the machine finally came out of use in 1988, and Alperton only has its stairs now). There has been little other change except at South Kensington where the lifts were withdrawn in September 1973, being replaced by a flight of three escalators to provide interchange with the District Line (and two further escalators, from January 1974, linking from an intermediate level directly to an enlarged District Line ticket hall).

Various investment programmes, especially those of the GLC, allowed the decor at many stations to be modernized in the 1980s: Finsbury Park, King's Cross, Holborn, Leicester Square, Piccadilly Circus, Green Park, South Kensington and Earl's Court all receiving modern finishings and designs at platform level, with some at ticket hall level too. A revival of interest in 1930s (and earlier) architecture also meant kindly 'restoration' of some of the 1906 and Holden style stations, or at least of some of the key features. A few platforms still portray the 1906 tile patterns, so characteristic of the line's opening.

During the 1970s and 1980s many central London stations were entirely refurbished, a number of decorative finishes having a local theme. At Leicester Square (celebrating local film connections) new metal panels around the entrances were found inconveniently large and subsequently set back (as seen left).

The District and Piccadilly station at Hammersmith occupied with other London Transport premises a huge amount of potential development land. On the other hand transport interchange was not ideal as the station found itself in the middle of a gyratory traffic system where any connection with local bus services was fraught with confusion and often required awkward road crossings, although a small bus station in Butterwick did its best to improve matters. After lengthy negotiation LT and a team of property developers gained planning permission to redevelop the site. The development included a huge shopping complex and a large bus station with escalator connections to the Underground station below; all local bus services were diverted via the new bus station, considerably improving transport links. Two new ticket halls replaced the old facilities, the north-west end ticket hall coming into service on 5th July 1993 and that at the south-east end on 12th September 1994; the bus station opened soon after, on 23rd October. At platform level the platforms themselves were largely unchanged and remained open to the air, though new awnings, stairways, facilities and equipment were provided.

There have been few major station works since the 1930s but Hillingdon stands out as an exception. The Metropolitan Railway wooden 'halt' had survived surprisingly unscathed since it opened in 1923 but during the 1980s found itself in the way of a scheme to re-route the A40 Oxford trunk road. The Department of Transport agreed to pay for shifting the platforms westwards for a bridge over the forthcoming road, and this required the entire station to be replaced by a modern glass and steel structure. Work began in January 1991 and the re-sited platforms came into use in July 1992, initially with access from the former entrance and old platform. The station access bridge came into use in December 1992 after which the old platforms could be demolished and the new rail bridge rolled into place; the station building was completed piecemeal during 1993. Works were not finally completed until 1994 when the passenger lifts were at last brought into regular use. Less major work at neighbouring Ickenham station in 1971 resulted in a neat modern ticket hall that replaced the ageing Metropolitan Railway hut.

At Knightsbridge the west end ticket hall became heavily congested by eager shoppers at certain times of the day and required major surgery. Work began in May 1999 with construction of a bridge over Brompton Road to allow work to take place underneath. The west end works had been completed by March 2005 and included a much-enlarged ticket hall and a new entrance within Hans Crescent, requiring it to be permanently closed to through traffic. Work then proceeded on modernizing the platforms and east end ticket hall.

A project causing considerable change to the public's perception of the Piccadilly was the huge amount of work undertaken from the end of 1986 to install the new systemwide Underground Ticketing System (UTS). The principal intention was to provide new high security ticket offices equipped with computerized ticket-issuing equipment and passenger-operated ticket machines which could be serviced from within the ticket office area. In central London, stations were equipped with automatic ticket gates to check all tickets on entry to and exit from the system, most stations in Zone 1 having gates by 1990. At outer stations the intention was for traditional ticket barriers to remain, the idea being that a thorough ticket check at one end of the journey coupled with the risk of a penalty fare being charged elsewhere was sufficient incentive to carry a correct ticket. In 1998 a private finance initiative was entered into with a commercial partner called Transaction Systems Ltd (or 'Transys') for upgrading the UTS system and introducing the smartcard technology now known as 'Oyster'. As part of this scheme nearly all stations have now been equipped with ticket gates or validating equipment. Most stations had gates fitted by 2000 though 16 remaining stations were fitted in 2001–03. The Oyster facility also required major changes to the equipment inside ticket offices. Transys comprises Cubic Transportation Systems, Electronic Data Systems, Fujitsu and W.S. Atkins; Cubic was also heavily involved in the original UTS installations.

A by-product of the new ticket system is that all the old-fashioned ticket offices became redundant. These included the free-standing booths known as Passimeters which characterize in particular the Holden stations. Under the Passimeter system the original idea was that the booking clerk at quiet times performed three operations: he issued tickets, checked tickets already held by inwards passengers, and checked or collected tickets of outwards passengers. This system became quite widespread in the 1920s and 1930s but largely fell into disuse after the war, although the booths remained for ticket issuing. Many booths still remain at listed stations, some adapted to new uses, such as retail. Some new ticket offices have been provided in the original external style, such as that at Covent Garden, but the structures are new.

An out-of-use Passimeter at Sudbury Town station, a Grade II listed building.

King's Cross station has already been the subject of considerable attention. The modernization of the Midland main line in the 1970s, and the improved services initially to Moorgate and thence via 'Thameslink', resulted in the re-invigoration of the moribund King's Cross (Widened Lines) station, now the bustling – perhaps too bustling – King's Cross Thameslink. This received a new ticket hall (managed by British Rail) in 1983, and a lengthy subway was built giving direct access to both the Victoria Line and Piccadilly Line platforms, the latter being reached by a set of stairs at the far end of the 1939 platform-level concourse.

In 1987 the station achieved somewhat less positive fame when it was the scene of a major fire which resulted in 31 deaths: a fire broke out beneath the main Piccadilly Line escalators and rapidly developed into an inferno of quite exceptional proportions. One result of this was a major review of all safety systems on the Underground, and amongst many other measures the systematic elimination of combustible finishes, and finishes which, whilst not combustible in themselves, are liable to give off smoke or dangerous fumes in the event of fire. This resulted in a vast quantity of station works in the early 1990s where station ceilings were removed or stripped of paint, and a plethora of fire protection cabling sprouted. By the late 1990s nearly all station works were complete and stations were all equipped with state-of-the-art fire protection and communications equipment. Staff procedures and training had also been drastically overhauled.

As a by-product, the fire drew unwelcome attention to the sheer inadequacy of old stations to deal efficiently with mounting traffic flows; King's Cross was more unsatisfactory than many in having a heavy interchange flow between the three tube lines and the Metropolitan Line that required travel outside the barrier lines between the two ticket halls. With the imminent arrival of the Channel Tunnel Rail Link at a reinvigorated St Pancras station, a major enlargement of the Underground ticket halls here was under way during the Piccadilly Line's centenary year.

King's Cross received unwelcome attention on 7th July 2005 when it was the scene of one of the four terrorist bomb attacks on London's transport during the morning rush hour which caused 56 deaths, over 500 injuries, virtually closed the capital for the rest of that day and disrupted the Underground for several weeks. The King's Cross incident occurred shortly after a westbound Piccadilly Line train had pulled away towards Russell Square when a suicide bomber set off a powerful bomb killing 26 victims, seriously injuring many others and writing off two carriages. Access to the site, in single track tube, was only available from either King's Cross or Russell Square and conditions for the rescuers and survivors were appalling. Services over this section could only be resumed on 3rd August. In the meantime, shuttle services operated between Arnos Grove and Cockfosters, Hyde Park Corner and Heathrow, and Acton Town and Rayners Lane.

Transfer of London Transport from the Minister of Transport to the Greater London Council in 1970 resulted in overall policy, including fares policy, being directed by the GLC, which could also provide funding support. Whilst under government control, grants for capital funding of public transport projects had been extremely rare, support generally only amounting to signing off loans of government money which were expected to be paid back, and upon which interest was due. During transfer to the GLC, London Transport's capital debt was written off saving huge interest payments each year and releasing investment funds to modernize the system; in addition, the GLC was willing to contribute to funding for improvements, providing projects were justifiable on a cost/benefit basis. From about 1972 the GLC came to be the principal source of capital investment but in turn LT had to try and contain operating costs within its fares revenue. This allowed a considerable amount of modernization to be undertaken, though much of it should really have been done much earlier and even today the backlog inherited from the 1940s and 1950s period of starvation is still evident.

In 1981–02 the GLC sought to reduce fares drastically to encourage a switch to public transport. Although the policy was implemented, the political and legal dispute that followed caused fares to double. Almost as a direct consequence of this 'Fare's Fair' debacle, the Government decided to abolish the GLC and as part of this process returned London Transport directly back to government control. It was not all bad news. The GLC then found itself in the curious position of making two huge fares reductions within two years and on each occasion took the opportunity first to introduce and then massively to expand zonal ticketing, out of which was born today's popular travelcard. This was really only feasible when fares reductions cushioned the effect on those whose journeys would otherwise have cost more, as zoning creates losers as well as winners. The transfer back to the Government was effected by the London Regional Transport Act 1984, which also renamed the governing board 'London Regional Transport' (LRT), though it soon insisted on rejuvenating the familiar 'London Transport' brand. The Act required LRT to manage its day-to-day operations through subsidiary companies and in 1985 the Underground assets and operations were established as a limited Company (London Underground Limited, or LUL), reporting to LRT. In 1988, the Piccadilly Line was established as a distinct management unit within the Underground, and for some years had complete day-to-day responsibility for its services and (from about 1991) most routine maintenance.

Change has soon overtaken this arrangement, partly resulting from the hurdles in obtaining adequate Government capital funding for the continued improvements that were necessary at a steady enough rate; when the Government took LT control from the GLC, it effectively committed itself to levels of funding at least broadly equivalent to those given by the GLC, and this it found itself uneasy about. At first, LUL was encouraged to identify a number of private finance initiatives (PFIs) to facilitate asset replacement. The Piccadilly Line therefore has (or will) enjoy benefits from new ticketing, power supply and communications systems. PFIs avoid up-front capital costs but have to be paid for through service charges instead. The 1997 Government decided to embark on something rather bigger and decided to 'PFI' the entire network, rebranding the process on the way through as the PPP, or public-private partnership. This was to vest for thirty years all trains and infrastructure in three infrastructure companies that would then be sold. In 1999 the Piccadilly Line trains, assets and associated engineers were transferred to an LUL-owned company called 'Infraco JNP', which also included the equivalent Northern and Jubilee Lines assets and staff. On 31st December 2002 Infraco JNP was sold to a company called Tube Lines, which was a consortium of Amey, Bechtel and Jarvis, though the last of these later pulled out. As part of this process LUL had to divest itself of its engineering capability which meant disentangling the line structures only recently put together, and putting a logical structure around what was left. The Piccadilly still has its own line management structure and is now run as part of what is known as JNP directorate – LUL staff still provide the operating capability to drive trains, manage stations and provide necessary head office services.

The Aldwych branch is no longer with us and it is perhaps surprising it survived as long as it did. Closure of the branch was sought in 1958 but it was reprieved, though economies were made with the abandonment of off-peak services from 7th June 1958. The Saturday morning 'peak' service remained until abandonment after the last train on 5th August 1962, by which time Saturday mornings no longer evidenced themselves as being part of the normal working week.

The branch was clearly unsatisfactory as a short shuttle service along a route well served with buses, and thoughts returned periodically to the possibility of extension to Waterloo, just across the Thames. Powers were obtained in 1965 for a double track extension, with a single terminal platform running directly beneath York Road. Working sites were identified, civil engineering planning completed and tenders were ready to be invited. The advantages of the extension included improving the distributing capacity of the Underground at Waterloo, as well as relieving the some heavily used sections of other lines. Formal application to the Minister of Transport was made in July 1965 for 'in principle' approval to build, but by 1968 no response had been forthcoming and the proposal was not pursued in that form; the Minister was no doubt influenced by the prevailing expenditure crisis, coupled with the relatively high costs of the scheme and the very poor return, even in social benefit terms (in a 1964 study, average time saving to Underground passengers was estimated at only two minutes). The extension's rationale was further demolished by the introduction in September 1968 of a network of frequent, limited stop, high capacity, single deck 'Red Arrow' bus services, no fewer than six of which were based on Waterloo. Four of the routes crossed Waterloo Bridge, with two passing Aldwych en route to the City and a third proceeding via Holborn station (in the northbound direction using the old tram subway which avoided the Aldwych traffic). On a short route buses had the huge time advantage of avoiding the need to descend into the depths of the earth, and at Waterloo they pulled up right outside the main-line station. At Holborn the interchange quality of the Aldwych branch with other lines was mostly poor and access to the street was very tedious. Buses such as Red Arrows could therefore achieve at very low cost what the tube extension could do less well at vast cost.

During the 1960s the proposed Fleet Line was to have had a substantial station at Aldwych and this would have absorbed the lower station area of the Aldwych branch station introducing a reasonable quality interchange, perhaps generating significant new traffic through new links and modern facilities. After three decades of vacillation, the Fleet (now Jubilee) Line routeing was much revised and the recent extension of that line goes nowhere near Aldwych (though the Jubilee Line Stage 1 over-run tunnels beyond Charing Cross come within a few hundred yards). By the end of 1968 London Transport was considering incorporating the Holborn–Aldwych branch into a possible north-east London to south-west London railway, which would have run via Waterloo. Aldwych would have become a double-ended station, with the southern entrance amalgamated with the nearby Temple station on the District Line. This line eventually came into public view as part of the 1973–74 London Rail Study, where it was announced as the 'Chelsea–Hackney Line'. However, during the late 1980s the proposed routeing was shifted north-westwards via Tottenham Court Road, leaving the Holborn–Aldwych branch to its fate.

Quite apart from the modest operating loss made by the branch, the question finally arose of the capital expenditure required if the line were to survive, and in particular the problem of the ageing lifts which failed to meet modern safety standards. It was difficult to make the case to divert scarce funding into the provision of new lifts at such a little used station (costs would have been over £3m). Notice was given in August 1993 of London Underground's desire to close the branch, and this resulted in a Public Inquiry in November 1993. Consent to closure was eventually given in August 1994, and an uncharacteristically packed last train ran on 30th September 1994. The lifts at Aldwych, though partially modernized in the early 1950s, were the last of the old Otis lifts on the Underground and were nearly 87 years old, a great testimony to their designers and a life impossible to achieve today. The disused station is retained as a training facility and commercial filming has also been undertaken there as it is well out of the way of passengers. The building looks likely to stay until property development in the area unlocks it from King's College which surrounds it on four faces as well as the basement and upper floors.

The conversion of trains to one-person operation on the Underground as a whole was a protracted affair. Nevertheless modification work to the 1973 stock was under way during 1986/87 and one-person operation was introduced on 31st August 1987. To reduce the risk of a train operator opening the doors on the wrong side of the train, it was considered necessary to equip each train with a 'correct side door enable' interlock circuit, which prevented the relevant passenger doors opening unless the train was correctly berthed alongside a platform; this work was undertaken between 1992 and 6th September 1993 when the system was commissioned.

During the 1990s the most significant visual development on the Piccadilly was the refurbishment of the 1973 stock, which gave rise to considerable thought. The spur for this was the King's Cross fire which caused LUL to review every material used below ground, including that used on the trains themselves. LUL concluded that for a train that was going to be around for many years it would be desirable to replace some internal materials and this presented an opportunity to completely modernize the interiors rather than simply replacing like for like. To test concepts, an initial unit was converted by Metro-Cammell and entered service on 20th January 1991.

Interior view of the 1973 stock after refurbishment by the Canadian company Bombardier in Doncaster. The seating layout was remodelled to give more space for luggage and to accommodate wheelchairs.

In June 1995 one train appeared painted in the external livery of United Airlines, incorporating a slogan along the side – the Underground's first all-over advertising train, an innovative way of increasing advertising income; the seat trim was replaced with the airline's own fabric design a few months later. During 1998, the train was despatched for refurbishment and came back in LUL corporate livery.

Increasing levels of train service began to push to the limit the amount of 1973 stock available each day, and some thought was given to increasing the size of the fleet by converting a number of displaced 1983 stock cars released from the Jubilee Line. A number of 3-car sets were put aside while the scheme was investigated but it was finally determined that conversion would be extremely expensive, especially the re-engineering of the car bodies to replace the single doorways by double doors at each centre bay. Major electrical works would also have been needed, and it is likely that the middle driving cabs would have had to be removed. Rolling stock availability has been increased through improved maintenance procedures but further train service increases will be difficult without more stock. Currently, the fleet size comprises 86 trains, seven cars of the original fleet have had to be scrapped for various reasons, and one serves as a track recording car. On the other hand the six cars comprising the experimental tube train were brought into fleet service during 1986–87.

Train service levels have varied enormously over the years following the opening of the eastern and western extensions, and it is convenient to review these now.

The Rayners Lane branch saw a slight decline in fortunes with overall traffic reductions over the years, though this has more recently been redressed. When the Piccadilly was formally projected westwards of South Harrow in 1933, a proportion of trains ran through to Uxbridge all day, every day. It must be recalled that at that time the area was developing extremely rapidly. During the war, as we saw, South Harrow diminished as a normal intermediate reversing point in favour of Rayners Lane. In 1956, to take an illustrative year, six trains an hour (a 10-minute service) operated midday off-peak to and from the Rayners Lane branch, and four of them went to and from Uxbridge, meshing in as best they could with the four trains an hour of the Metropolitan Line. From 2nd March 1959 the midday Piccadilly off-peak service beyond Rayners Lane was curtailed, though evening off-peak services (and those all day Saturdays and Sundays) continued. From 16th October 1967 the evening off-peak and the Sunday through trains disappeared, followed by Saturday afternoon and evening trains from 30th November 1970. The Saturday morning service went in 1974. In contrast, the Metropolitan services on the Uxbridge branch had remained fairly static. A couple of individual Piccadilly workings west of Rayners Lane survived on Sundays for some years, but these last ran on 27th October 1991.

Through Piccadilly trains to and from Uxbridge ran continuously during the Monday-Friday peaks, not always entirely regularly and with overall reductions over the years. Again, in 1956 there were nine through morning trains from Uxbridge (or Hillingdon) in the busiest hour, joined by a further seven from Rayners Lane and another one from South Harrow – 17 trains in all. By 1970 there were still nine trains from Uxbridge, with a further five from Rayners Lane (14 in all). In 1980 there were seven trains from Uxbridge/Hillingdon, a further four from Ruislip and four more from Rayners Lane (15 in all, a marginal overall improvement, especially between Rayners Lane and Ruislip). From May 1994 there were 13 trains (five trains from Uxbridge, four from Ruislip and four from Rayners Lane), though the service had just been enhanced from an all-time low of ten trains, which had proved insufficient.

On the Hounslow branch the position was more stable, though the loss of the District service in 1964 was hardly compensated by Piccadilly improvement. In 1956 there were eleven Piccadilly and seven District trains from Hounslow in the peak hour, plus two more Piccadilly trains from Northfields – 20 trains from the branch as a whole. Off-peak there was a 10-minute Piccadilly-only service from Hounslow. A decade later there were just fourteen Piccadilly trains in the peak hour, all from Hounslow, still with a 10-minute off-peak interval. By 1980 there were still fourteen Piccadilly trains in the peak hour, all now from Heathrow, but off-peak services had been boosted to two trains every ten minutes.

In recent times train service levels have increased dramatically, especially off-peak and weekend services. This is partly a result of London's buoyant economy (especially tourism) coupled with a fares policy designed to switch more travel onto public transport. Oyster cards and road congestion charging have helped further.

2006 services required 76 trains for peak operation and 65 off-peak. Central London peak intervals were 2½ minutes, just 24 trains an hour, a far lower intensity than had been run half a century previously but the most that can presently be managed whilst maintaining essential reliability; the peaks are also more spread than in years gone by, which requires a less intense service. During the peaks an approximate 5-minute service operates between Acton Town and Rayners Lane, with two out of three trains proceeding to and from Ruislip and one out of three to or from Uxbridge. On the Heathrow branch a 5-minute service (just 12 trains an hour) is maintained to and from the airport.

During the Monday-Friday off-peak a 5-minute pattern is maintained to and from Heathrow with a 10-minute service to Rayners Lane with alternate trains proceeding to and from Uxbridge, which gets a 20-minute service. All these trains now go to Cockfosters at the east end of the line. To improve intervals through central London a further three trains an hour operate between Northfields and Arnos Grove; the combined central London off-peak service is therefore a curious 21 trains an hour. In 1996 a 24 trains an hour off-peak service had been introduced requiring 69 trains – the most intense ever – but it was found very difficult to operate and had to be eased back to 21 an hour with 65 trains.

In 1998, BAA plc (Heathrow's owner) opened 'Heathrow Express', an express train service to Paddington using a new link from the GW main line near Hayes. This serves the central area terminals at one station and Terminal 4 at a second (terminal) station. Intended mainly for the premium market, and perhaps suffering from an imperfectly located terminus at Paddington, outside the main tourist and business districts, the service did not impact too heavily on Piccadilly Line traffic.

It is worth recalling that even while the Heathrow Terminal 4 extension was still on the drawing board, a further public inquiry was in progress to examine the case for a fifth airline terminal – this turned out to be the UK's longest ever planning enquiry and from the development submission on 17th February 1993 the inspector's positive recommendation did not emerge until 1999, nearly four years after the enquiry began in May 1995. Ministerial approval was not forthcoming until 20th November 2001 and work finally began the following year. The scale is enormous, the entire terminal and new aircraft movement area being about the size of Hyde Park. Construction on such a scale requires excellent transport provision, and as part of the planning process BAA agreed to fund an extension of the Piccadilly Line to the new terminal, as well as extension of Heathrow Express.

The new terminal, to London Underground's frustration, is on the old Perry Oaks sludge works site originally thought likely to have been the home of Terminal 4, and its location now makes it impossible for any one Piccadilly train to serve all three terminal areas; had this been known when Terminal 4 was being planned, then it would have been done differently. Various ideas were considered to make the best of a bad job, including another station on the loop and a long people mover. In the end the least worst option was to build a twin track extension from Heathrow Terminals 1,2,3 to a new station at Terminal 5, but retain a junction with the loop west of Heathrow 1,2,3 so that a proportion of the service could still serve Terminal 4.

To enable the junctions west of Heathrow Terminals 1,2,3 to be built it was necessary to close the Terminal 4 loop between 7th January 2005 and 17th September 2006, during which time trains ran direct between Hatton Cross and Terminals 1,2,3 along the old route. A bus service was put on between Terminal 4 and Hatton Cross, and in the London-bound direction this often made for a quicker journey than the train would have done.

To keep pace with demand, the Piccadilly Line will need to see enhanced train frequencies and improved reliability. One constraint to this has been the inadequate reversing facilities at the east end of the line. When opened in 1932/33 it was felt that a significant proportion of the service could turn short of Cockfosters at Wood Green and Arnos Grove. In practice it is impossible to use Wood Green siding as a reversing point without causing serious delays to trains behind, and in any case it is now too close to central London to offer much benefit. Arnos Grove has only a centre platform for reversing and realistically could be expected to turn perhaps one train in four. To improve service reliability, layovers of at least eight minutes are needed and this is barely achievable with current levels, so enhanced services ideally require at least one and perhaps two additional reversing platforms at this end of the line.

BAA diagram of tunnelling relating to Terminal 5. Quite how traffic will ultimately distribute itself around the terminals is open to question but as Terminal 5 is far larger than the other terminals put together the general drift can be inferred.

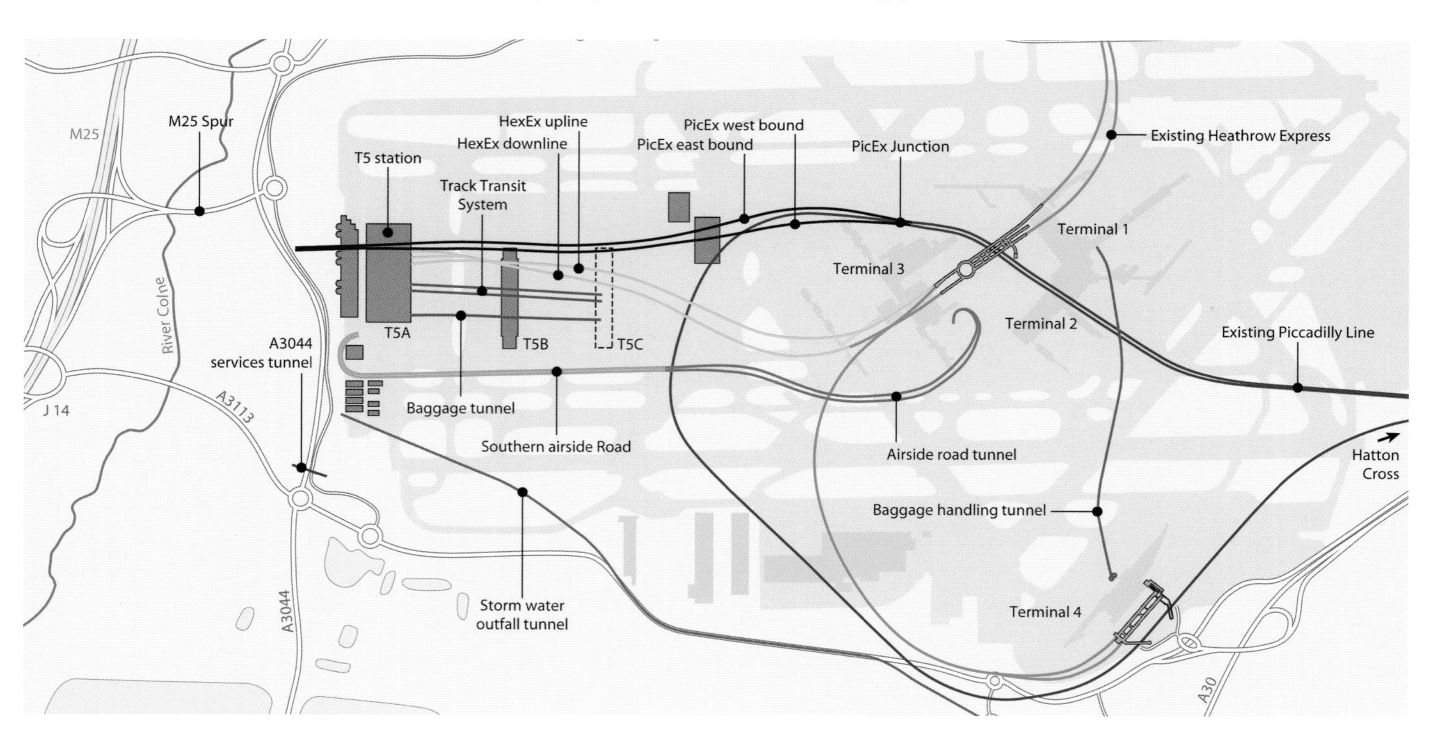

Part of the ticket hall at Heathrow Terminal 5 station.

Under the PPP relationship with Tube Lines, the Piccadilly will benefit from a new signalling system and an entirely new fleet of trains. This scheme is planned for completion in 2014 and will involve provision of 93 new trains and signalling designed to increase capacity by 35 per cent and journey times by 16 per cent over the line as a whole. Such a system is likely to involve automatic train operation as this makes it easier to achieve optimal speeds and train intervals. The existing control room at Earl's Court, serving both District and Piccadilly Lines, is old and cramped, and it is proposed to build a modern control room for these lines close to the new Train Operating Centre at Acton Town, recently constructed.

Tube Lines has promised to modernize ten stations and refurbish a further 25, some of which have already been done, such as Caledonian Road where the original tiled finishes have been carefully repaired. All lifts and eighteen escalators will be refurbished with a further eleven escalators replaced. PPP contractors are not specifically committed to additional major works at stations but London Underground can require major upgrades if it feels works are justified and is prepared to pay for them.

For the future the Piccadilly Line stations face some challenges. Increasing traffic levels may create some serious congestion problems at key stations, notably Finsbury Park, Russell Square, Holborn, Covent Garden and Piccadilly Circus. Some of these stations are already under stress and Covent Garden is in great difficulty already during evenings and at weekends even though old passages were reopened and additional lifts installed as the market area became a tourist attraction in the 1980s; even today the station has to be closed to incoming passengers at certain times – mitigation measures are currently under discussion for enlarging the James Street exit with additional ticket gates and circulating space outside the lifts. A much larger scheme involving a new ticket hall on a different site is also under development.

Plans for reconstruction or enhancement of other stations to a greater or lesser degree have been in hand for each of these locations but the timing and the extent to which these are taken forward (if at all) will depend on available funding, developing traffic patterns, local developments in the area, the impact of any new lines and, of course, the ability to cope with prevailing traffic safely in the interim. Other significant factors during the next ten years will be the desire to provide better access for disabled people (implying greater lift provision, probably in addition to escalators), and yet greater levels of passenger security. Activity at Heathrow needs to settle down after Terminal 5 opening, once the planned long-term redevelopment of the central terminal buildings is complete and the very long-term future of Terminal 4 can be ascertained – the possibility of a Piccadilly Line shuttle to Terminal 4 has even been mooted as a better option than infrequent ex-London trains.

The Piccadilly Line has grown through three phases: its original opening phase, the 1930s expansion and reconstruction, and the Heathrow era. It is not only a very busy line, but in serving Heathrow it is possibly the most well-known London Underground line in the world.

At Leicester Square station, London Underground Managing Director Tim O'Toole holds a large Birthday card at a celebration of the Piccadilly Line's centenary on 15th December 2006.

INDEX

Note: There may be more than one reference on the page indicated.